TECHNICAL DRAWING
FOR G.C.E. & C.S.E.

TECHNICAL DRAWING FOR G.C.E. & C.S.E.

J. N. GREEN

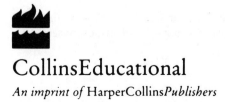

CollinsEducational

An imprint of HarperCollins*Publishers*

This edition 1992 by
CollinsEducational
77-85 Fulham Palace Road
Hammersmith, London W6 8JB

www.**Collins**Education.com
On-line Support for Schools and Colleges

Reprinted 1992, 1993, 1994, 1996, 1997, 1998, 1999, 2000, 2001, 2002

First published in 1964 by Allman & Sons Ltd
later incorporated in Mills & Boon Ltd
Third metric edition 1974
Reprinted 1975, 1976, 1977, 1978, 1980, 1982,
1983, 1984, 1985, 1986
Published by Unwin Hyman Limited 1988

British Library Cataloguing in Publication Data

Green, J. N.
    Technical drawing for GCE & CSE. – 3rd metric ed.
    1. Mechanical drawing – Problems, exercises, etc.
    I. Title
    604'.2'4076   T354

ISBN 0 00 322298 5

Printed by Martins the Printers Ltd, Berwick-upon-Tweed

CONTENTS

INTRODUCTION

This book is specially designed to meet the needs of pupils studying for the G.C.E. ('O' Level) and the C.S.E. and is a class textbook arranged in progressive stages. The first half comprises the plane and solid geometry and the second half the engineering drawing. The text has been reduced to a minimum to place greater emphasis on the drawings, thus enabling the pupil to learn quickly by active work.

It is hoped that the book will help many pupils to pass the examinations. The book is admirably suited for home study as well as for school use, and is planned to stimulate the natural interest and enthusiasm of the pupil for creative work.

A B C D E F G H I J K L M
N O P Q R S T U V W X Y Z

1 2 3 4 5 6 7 8 9 0

LETTERING

Good lettering and neat linework are very pleasing to look at on a drawing, and constant practice aimed .at producing plain, clear figures will result in the attainment of a good standard.

Always print between two construction lines.

In the early stages it is an advantage to pencil in the letters lightly with the aid of a ruler and then line in by hand.

TYPES OF LINES

Thick line for outlines.

Thin line for dimension lines, projection lines construction lines, hatching lines.

Thin short dashes for hidden detail.

Thin long chain for centre lines, pitch circles, path lines for indicating movement.

Thick long chain for cutting planes and viewing planes.

Ruled line and short zig-zags for long break lines.

Thick wavy line for short break lines and irregular boundary lines.

9

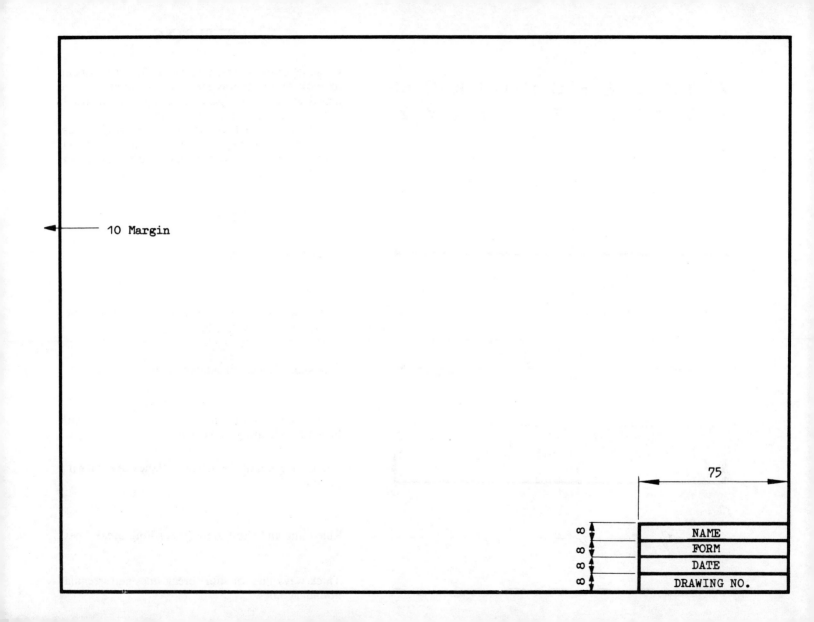

10 Margin

75

NAME

FORM

DATE

DRAWING NO.

8 8 8 8

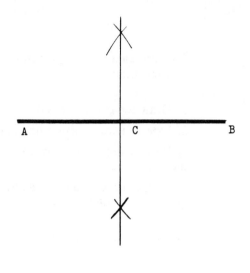

To Bisect a Given Line

1. Draw the given line AB.

2. With centre A and any radius greater than half AB draw arcs above and below the line.

3. With centre B draw arcs of the same radius to cut the previous ones.

4. The line drawn through the intersections of the arcs will bisect the given line AB at C.

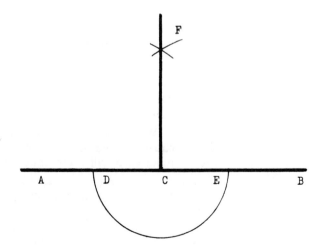

To Construct a Perpendicular at a Given Point on a Straight Line

1. Draw the given line AB.

2. Mark the given point C.

3. With centre C and any convenient radius draw the semicircle DE.

4. With centres D and E and any convenient radius draw arcs to intersect at F.

5. A line drawn from C through the intersection of the arcs is the perpendicular.

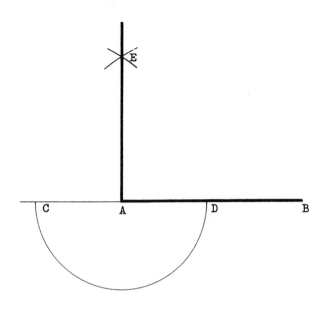

To Construct a Perpendicular at the End of a Given Line

1. Draw the given line AB.

2. Extend a construction line outwards from A.

3. With centre A and any convenient radius draw the semicircle CD.

4. With centres C and D and any convenient radius draw arcs to intersect at E.

5. A line drawn from A through the intersection of the arcs is the perpendicular.

To Draw a Parallel Line

1. Draw the line AB. Mark points 1 and 3 near to the ends of the line and point 2 about the centre of the line.

2. With centres 1, 2, 3 and a radius equal to the distance away of the required parallel line draw arcs.

3. A line drawn across the tops of the arcs is the required parallel line.

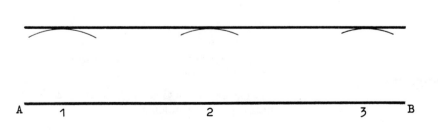

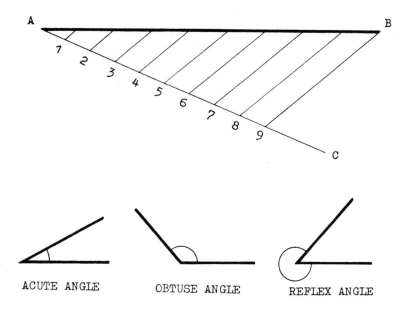

To Divide a Straight Line into a Given Number of Equal Parts

1. Draw the given line AB.

2. Draw line AC at any convenient angle to AB.

3. Step off along AC the required number of divisions. These may be of any convenient length, but equal.

4. Join the last number to point B. Draw lines parallel to this line from the other numbers. AB is now divided into the required number of equal parts.

ANGLES

When two lines meet they form an angle.

An acute angle is less than 90°; an obtuse angle is greater than 90° and less than 180°; a reflex angle is greater than 180°.

Angles are measured in degrees. There are 360° in a circle. Angles can be constructed and measured with a protractor.

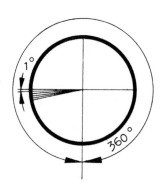

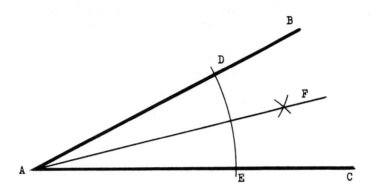

To Bisect a Given Angle

1. Draw the given angle BAC.

2. With centre A and any convenient radius draw an arc to cut AB at D and AC at E.

3. With centre D and any radius draw an arc.

4. With centre E and the same radius draw an arc to intersect the previous one at F.

5. Join AF. This is the bisector.

To Construct an Angle Similar to a Given Angle

1. Draw the given angle BAC. With centre A and any radius draw an arc to cut AB at D and AC at E.

2. Draw line FG. With centre F and radius AD draw an arc to cut FG at H.

3. With centre H and radius ED draw an arc to cut the previous one at J. Join FJ. Angle JFG is the similar angle.

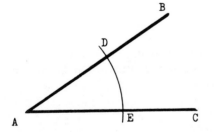
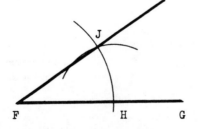

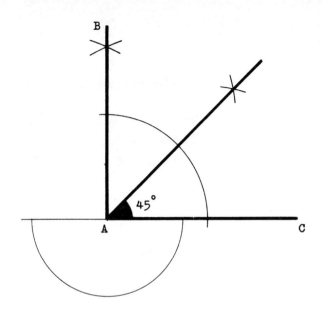

To Construct an Angle of 45°

1. Construct a right angle BAC (as on page 12).
2. Bisect the right angle to obtain a 45° angle.

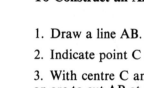

To Construct an Angle of 60°

1. Draw a line AB.

2. Indicate point C anywhere on AB.

3. With centre C and any convenient radius draw an arc to cut AB at D.

4. With centre D and the same radius draw an arc to cut the previous one at E.

5. Draw a line from C through E (line CF). FCB is the required 60° angle.

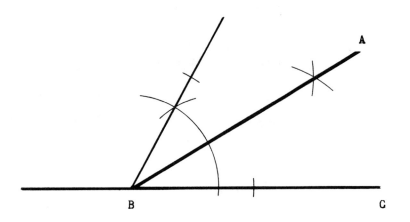

To Construct an Angle of 30°

1. Construct an angle of 60°, as on page 15.
2. Bisect the 60° angle.
3. Angle ABC is the required 30° angle.

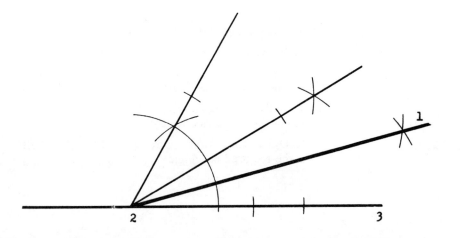

To Construct an Angle of 15°

1. Construct an angle of 30°, as above.
2. Bisect the 30° angle.
3. Angle 1, 2, 3 is the required 15° angle.

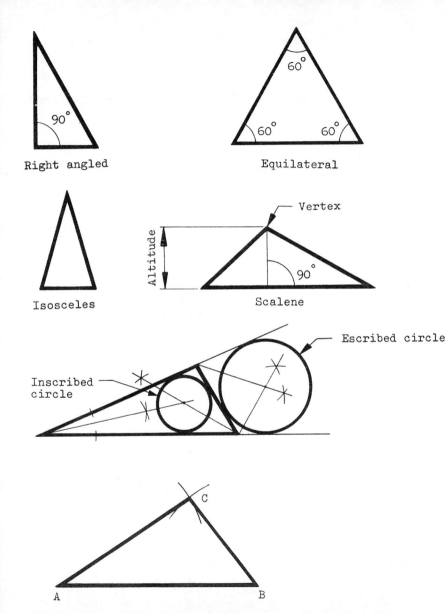

Right angled

Equilateral

Isosceles

Vertex

Altitude

Scalene

90°

Escribed circle

Inscribed circle

TRIANGLES

A triangle is a plane rectilineal figure with 3 sides. A right-angled triangle has 1 angle 90°. The side opposite the right angle is called the hypotenuse. An equilateral triangle has 3 equal sides and angles. An isosceles triangle has 2 equal sides and angles. A scalene triangle has 3 unequal sides and angles.

To Construct any Triangle Given the Length of the Three Sides

1. Draw one side AB.

2. With centre A and a radius of one of the remaining sides draw an arc.

3. With centre B and a radius of the remaining side draw an arc to intersect the previous one at C.

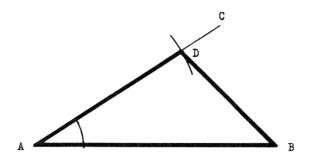

To Draw a Triangle when Given Two Sides and the Included Angle

1. Draw one given side AB.

2. Construct the included angle CAB.

3. With centre A and a radius of the other given side draw an arc to cut AC at D.

4. Join AD and DB. DAB is the required triangle.

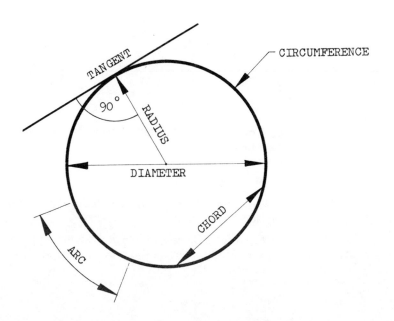

THE CIRCLE

A circle is a plane figure bounded by a curved line called the circumference, which is always equidistant from the centre.

A diameter is a straight line drawn through the centre, meeting the circumference at both ends.

A radius is a straight line drawn from the centre to the circumference.

An arc is any part of the circumference.

A chord is any straight line drawn across the circle, meeting the circumference at both ends.

A tangent is a straight line which touches the circumference. It is always at right angles to the radius.

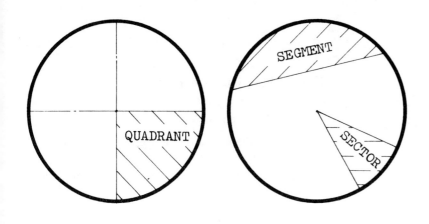

A segment is part of a circle bounded by an arc and a chord.

A sector is part of a circle bounded by two radii and an arc.

A quadrant is part of a circle bounded by two radii at right angles and an arc.

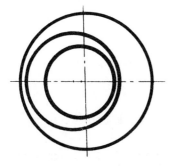

Eccentric Circles

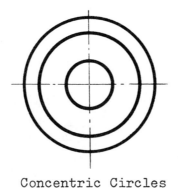

Concentric Circles

Concentric circles have the same centre but different radii.

Eccentric circles have different centres.

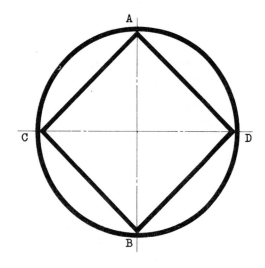

To Inscribe a Square in a Circle

1. Draw the given circle.

2. Draw the diameters AB and CD at right angles to each other.

3. Draw lines AC, CB, BD and DA, to complete the square.

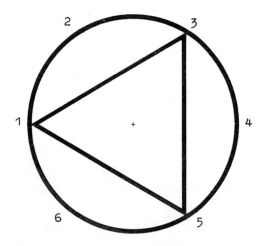

To Inscribe an Equilateral Triangle in a Circle

1. Draw the given circle.

2. Take the radius of the circle and step it off six times on the circumference.

3. Join every second point on the circumference to complete the equilateral triangle.

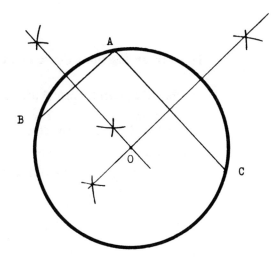

To Find the Centre of a Circle

1. Draw any two chords AB and AC.

2. Bisect AB and AC. The bisecting lines intersect at O, which is the centre of the circle.

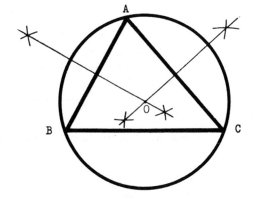

To Draw the Circumscribed Circle to a Given Triangle

1 Draw the given triangle ABC.

2. Bisect any two sides. The bisecting lines intersect at O, which is the centre of the required circle.

3. With centre O and radius OA draw the circle which will also pass through B and C.

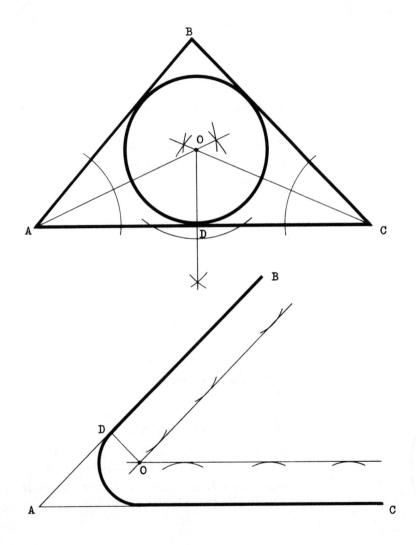

To Draw an Inscribed Circle to a Given Triangle

1. Draw the given triangle ABC.

2. Bisect any two angles. The bisecting lines will intersect at O, which is the centre of the circle.

3. Draw a perpendicular to any side from O.

4. With centre O and radius OD draw the required circle.

To Draw a Circle or Arc of Given Radius to Touch Two Given Converging Lines

1. Draw the given lines AB and AC.

2. Draw lines parallel to AB and AC at a distance equal to the radius of the required circle, to intersect at O.

3. Draw a line perpendicular to AB from O (line OD).

4. With centre O and radius OD draw the arc.

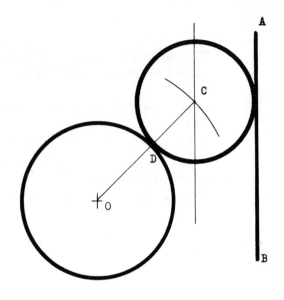

To Draw a Circle of Given Radius to Touch a Given Straight Line and Circle

1. Draw the given straight line AB and circle with centre O.

2. Draw a line parallel to AB at a distance equal to the radius of the required circle.

3. Take the length, radius of required circle + radius of given circle, and with O as a centre draw an arc to cut the parallel line at C.

4. With centre C and radius CD draw the required circle.

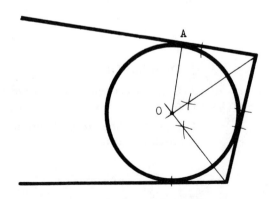

To Draw a Circle to Touch Three Given Lines

1. Draw the three given lines.

2. Bisect the two angles. The bisecting lines intersect at O, the centre of the required circle.

3. Draw a line (OA) perpendicular to any side from O.

4. With centre O and radius OA draw the required circle.

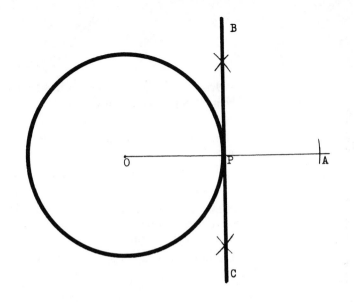

To Construct a Tangent to a Circle at a Given Point on the Circumference

1. Draw the circle with centre O. Indicate the given point P.

2. Extend a line from OP outwards.

3. With centre P and radius OP draw an arc to cut the extended line at A.

4. Bisect OA. The bisector BC is the required tangent.

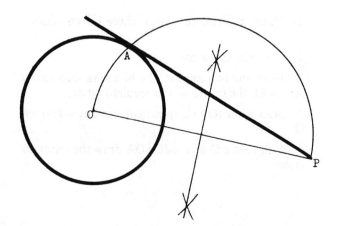

To Construct a Tangent to a Circle from a Given Point Outside it

1. Draw the circle with centre O. Indicate the given point P.

2. Draw line OP.

3. Construct a semicircle on OP to cut the circle at A.

4. Extend a line from P through A. This is the required tangent.

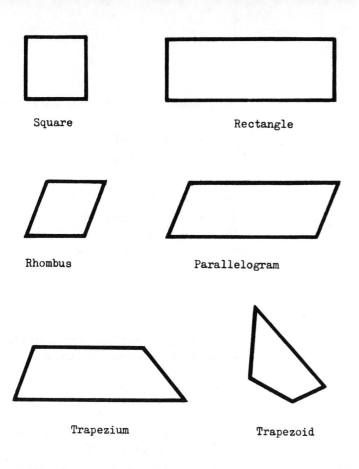

Square

Rectangle

Rhombus

Parallelogram

Trapezium

Trapezoid

Deltoid

QUADRILATERALS

A quadrilateral is a 4-sided plane figure.

A square has 4 equal sides. All its angles are right angles.

A rectangle has its opposite sides equal, and all its angles are right angles.

A rhombus has all its sides equal. Its angles are other than right angles.

A parallelogram has its opposite sides equal. Its angles are other than right angles.

A trapezium has 2 opposite sides parallel.

A trapezoid has 4 unequal sides and angles.

A deltoid or kite has its adjacent pairs of sides of equal length.

25

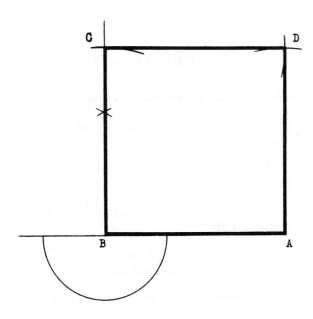

To Construct a Square Given the Length of Side

1. Draw one side AB.

2. Construct a right angle at B.

3. With centre B and a radius of the side draw an arc to cut the perpendicular at C.

4. With centres A and C in turn and a radius of the side draw arcs to intersect at D.

5. Join CD and DA to complete the square.

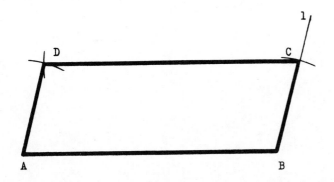

To Construct a Parallelogram Given the Length of the Two Sides and One Angle

1. Draw one side AB.

2. Construct the given angle AB1.

3. With centre B and a radius of the other side draw an arc to cut B1 at C.

4. With centre A and radius BC draw an arc.

5. With centre C and radius AB draw an arc to cut the previous one at D.

6. Join AD and DC.

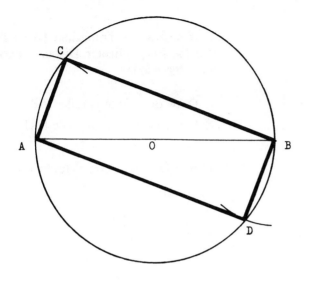

To Construct a Rectangle Given the Length of the Diagonal and One Side

1. Draw the diagonal AB and construct a circle on it.

2. With centre A and a radius of the given side draw an arc to cut the circumference at C.

3. With centre B and a radius of the given side draw an arc to cut the circumference at D.

4. Join AC, CB, BD and DA to complete the rectangle.

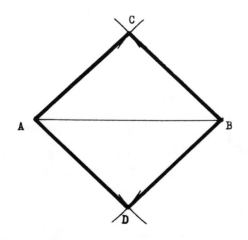

To Construct a Rhombus Given the Length of the Diagonal and Side

1. Draw the diagonal AB.

2. With centres A and B in turn and radius of side draw arcs above the line to intersect at C.

3. With centres A and B in turn and radius of side draw arcs below the line to intersect at D.

4. Join AC, CB, BD and DA to complete the rhombus.

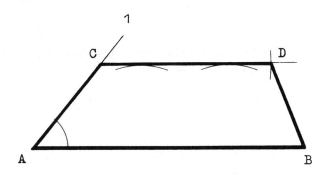

To Construct a Trapezium Given the Parallels and the Perpendicular Distance Between Them, and One Angle

1. Draw one of the parallels AB.
2. Construct the given angle BA1.
3. Draw the parallel CD.
4. Join D to B to complete the trapezium.

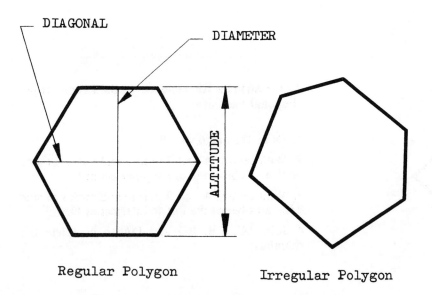

Regular Polygon

Irregular Polygon

POLYGONS

A polygon is a plane rectilineal figure with more than 4 sides.

Regular polygons have equal sides and angles.

A pentagon has 5 sides, a hexagon 6, a heptagon 7, an octagon 8, a nonagon 9 and a decagon 10.

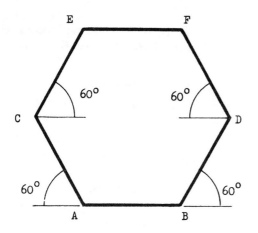

To Draw a Hexagon Using a 60° Set Square when Given the Length of Side

1. Draw one side AB.

2. Draw a line from A and B in turn at 60° and mark off the length of side to give points C and D.

3. Draw a line from C and D in turn at 60° and mark off the length of side to give points E and F.

4. Join E to F.

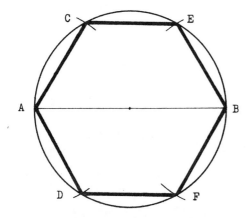

To Draw a Hexagon Within a Circle when Given the Length of Side

1. Draw a circle of radius equal to the length of the given side.

2. Draw horizontal diameter AB. With centres A and B in turn and radius of the circle draw arcs above and below AB to cut the circumference at C, D, E and F.

3. Join all the points to complete the hexagon.

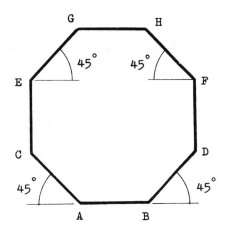

To Draw an Octagon Using a 45° Set Square when Given the Length of Side

1. Draw one side AB.

2. Draw a line from A and B in turn at 45° and mark off the length of side to give points C and D.

3. Draw a line from C and D in turn perpendicular to AB and mark off the length of side to give points E and F.

4. Draw a line from E and F in turn at 45° and mark off the length of side to give points G and H.

5. Join G to H.

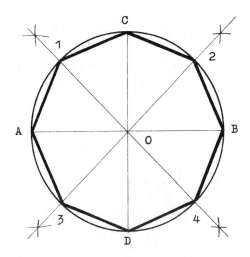

To Draw an Octagon Within a Given Circle

1. Draw the given circle with diameters AB and CD at right angles.

2. Bisect each of the 90° angles to give points 1, 2, 3 and 4 on the circumference.

3. Join all the points to complete the octagon.

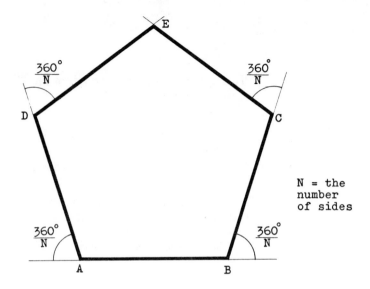

To Draw any Regular Polygon with the aid of a Protractor when given the Length of Side

1. Divide 360° by the number of sides (N) of the polygon to obtain the external angle. In this exercise a pentagon is to be constructed, therefore the external angle $=\dfrac{360°}{5}=72°$.

2. Draw one side AB and draw a construction line at 72° to AB from A and B. Mark the length of side, C and D, on these lines and draw lines at 72° to the sides BC and AD from C and D to intersect at E.

ABCED is the required pentagon.

To Circumscribe a Circle with any Regular Polygon

1. Divide 360° by the number of sides (N) of the polygon to obtain the internal angle. In this exercise the circle is to be circumscribed with a pentagon, therefore the internal angle $=\dfrac{360°}{5}=72°$.

2. Draw the circle with centre O. Draw a radius O1 and then construct the five angles of 72° at the centre O (angles 1O2, 2O3, etc.).

3. Draw AB to touch the circumference at 1 and perpendicular to O1, etc.

ABCDE is the required pentagon.

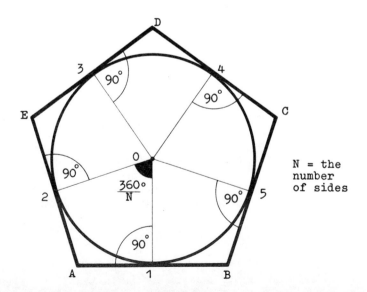

N = the number of sides

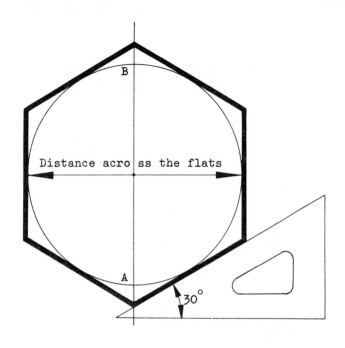

To Draw a Hexagon when Given the Distance Across the Flats

1. Draw a circle equal in diameter to the distance across the flats.

2. Draw an extended vertical diameter AB as shown.

3. Draw the four sides as shown with the set square, to touch the circumference of the circle. Draw the remaining two sides vertical and touching the circumference of the circle.

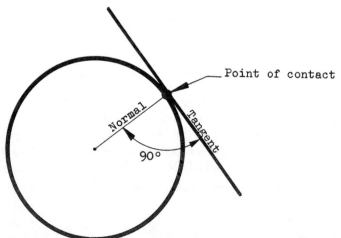

Point of Contact and a Normal

The point where the tangent touches the circumference of the circle is called 'the point of contact'. The radius joining the point of contact to the centre of the circle is called the 'normal'.

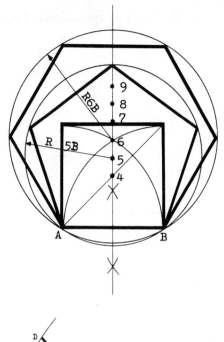

To Draw a Square and Polygons on a Given Base

1. Draw the given base AB and bisect it. Construct a square on AB. Draw a diagonal on the square to cut the bisector of AB at 4. With centres A and B in turn and radius AB draw arcs to intersect at 6. Bisect 4–6 to obtain point 5. Take unit 4–5 and step it off to obtain points 7, 8, 9, etc.

2. To draw the pentagon, use 5 as a centre and radius 5B and draw a circle. Take the Base AB and step it off on the circle to obtain the other four sides. Proceed in a similar manner to draw the other polygons with 6, 7, 8, etc. as the circle centres.

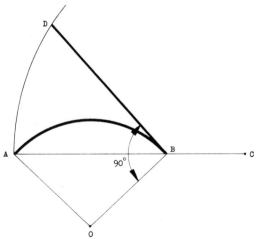

To Draw a Straight Line of Approximate Length to a Given Arc

1. Draw the given arc AB. Draw the chord from A to B and extend it to C, making BC equal to half AB.

2. Join A and B to the arc centre O. With centre C and radius CA draw an arc. Draw a line at right angles to OB from B to touch the arc at D. DB is the line of approximate length to the arc AB.

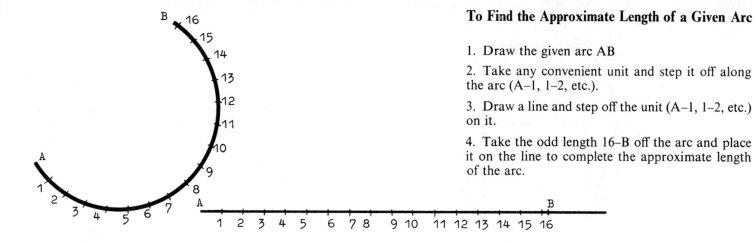

To Find the Approximate Length of a Given Arc

1. Draw the given arc AB

2. Take any convenient unit and step it off along the arc (A–1, 1–2, etc.).

3. Draw a line and step off the unit (A–1, 1–2, etc.) on it.

4. Take the odd length 16–B off the arc and place it on the line to complete the approximate length of the arc.

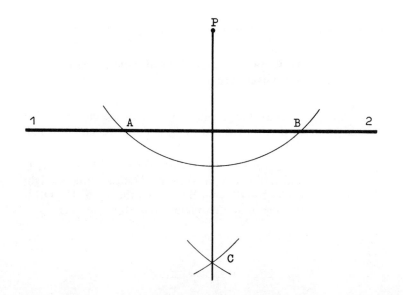

To Draw a Perpendicular to a Line from a Point Outside the Line

1. Draw the given line 1–2 and the given point P.

2. With centre P and any convenient radius draw an arc to cut the line at A and B.

3. With centres A and B in turn and any convenient radius draw arcs to intersect at C.

4. Draw a line from P through C. This is the perpendicular to the line.

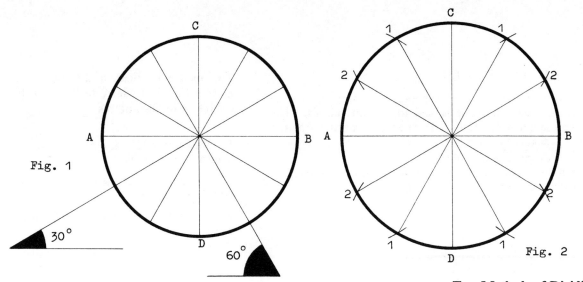

Fig. 1

30°

60°

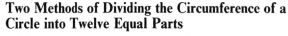

Fig. 2

Two Methods of Dividing the Circumference of a Circle into Twelve Equal Parts

Figure 1

1. Draw the horizontal diameter AB.

2. Draw diameter CD perpendicular to AB.

3. Use the 60° and the 30° angle of the set-square through the centre of the circle, this will give the required points on the curve.

Figure 2

1. Draw the diameters AB and CD perpendicular to each other.

2. With centres A, B, C, D, in turn and a radius of the given circle as a radius, draw the arcs 1 and 2.

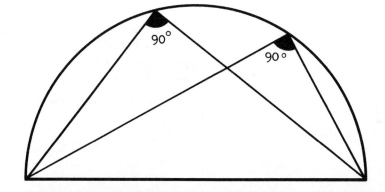

90°

90°

The Angle in a Semicircle is a Right Angle

PLAIN SCALES

An object is often too large to be drawn full size on paper, so a convenient scale is used. If an object is drawn half size, the scale is said to be half full size. The fraction $\frac{1}{2}$ is known as the representative fraction, R.F. The representative fraction

$$= \frac{\text{distance drawn}}{\text{distance represented}}.$$

A plain scale has two units of measurements, e.g. metres and decimetres. The scale used should always be stated on the drawing.

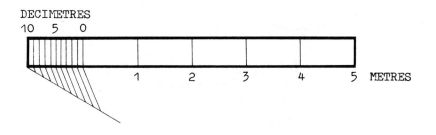

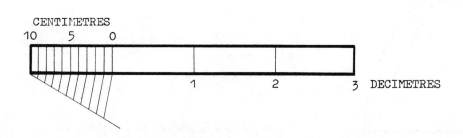

To Construct a Scale of 2 Centimetres Equals 1 Metre to Read up to 6 Metres in Decimetres

1. Draw a line 120 mm long and divide it into 20 mm units.

2. The height of the scale can be any convenient height.

3. Divide the first unit into 10 equal parts.

To Construct a Scale of 3 Centimetres Equals 1 Decimetre to Read up to 4 Decimetres in Centimetres

1. Draw a line 120 mm long and divide it into 4 equal parts.

2. The height of the scale can be any convenient height.

3. Divide the first unit into 10 equal parts.

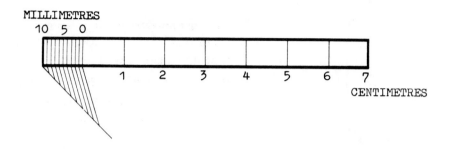

To Construct a Scale of 1½ Times Full Size to Read up to 8 Centimetres in Millimetres

1. Draw a line 120 mm long (1½ × 8 centimetres) and divide it into 8 equal units.

2. The height of the scale can be any convenient height.

3. Divide the first unit into 10 equal parts.

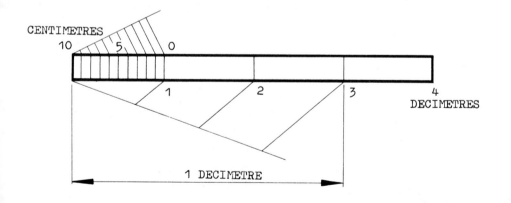

To Construct a Scale of ⅓ to Read up to 4 Decimetres in Centimetres

1. Draw a line 1 decimetre long and divide it into 3 equal parts. Each of these will represent a decimetre on the scale. Step off one of these parts to give the required 4 decimetres.

2. Divide the first part into 10 equal parts.

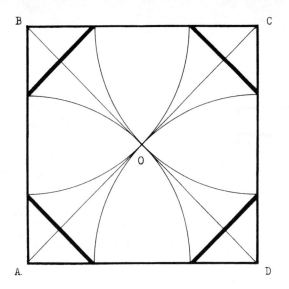

To construct an Octagon in a Square

1. Draw the square ABCD.

2. Draw diagonals AC and BD to intersect at O.

3. With centre A and radius AO draw an arc to touch the sides of the square. Repeat this for centres B, C and D.

4. Connect the points on the side of the square to complete the octagon.

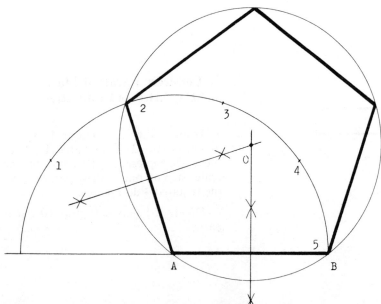

General Method for Constructing any Polygon when Given the Length of Side

1. Draw one side AB and extend it to the left.

2. With centre A and radius AB draw a semicircle and divide it by trial into as many equal parts as the required polygon has sides.

3. Draw A2. This is the second side of the required polygon in every example.

4. Bisect AB and A2. The bisectors intersect at O.

5. With centre O and radius OA draw a circle and mark off the 3 other sides of the polygon on it.

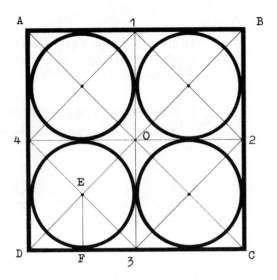

To Inscribe Four Equal Circles in a Square, Each to Touch Two Sides and Two Other Circles

1. Draw the given square.

2. Draw the diagonals AC and BD.

3. Through the intersection of the diagonals at O draw perpendiculars to the sides, 1–3, 2–4.

4. Draw diagonals 1–2, 2–3, 3–4, 4–1.

5. Draw EF perpendicular to side DC from E.

6. With radius EF and the intersections of the short diagonals as centres draw the four circles.

To Inscribe Four Equal Circles in a Square, Each to Touch One Side and Two Other Circles

1. Draw the given square.

2. Draw diagonals AC and BD.

3. Through the intersection of the diagonals at O draw perpendiculars to the sides, 1–3, 2–4.

4. Bisect angle OD3 to give centre E.

5. With centre O and radius OE mark the remaining three centres on the perpendiculars.

6. With radius E3 and each of the centres draw the four circles.

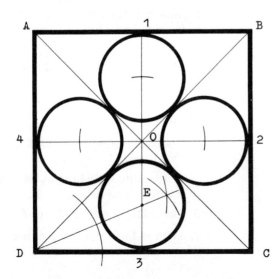

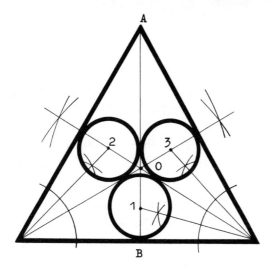

To Inscribe Three Equal Circles in an Equilateral Triangle, Each Circle to Touch One Side and Two Other Circles

1. Draw the given equilateral triangle.

2. Bisect two of the angles to determine the centre of the triangle, O.

3. Draw a line from A through O to B.

4. Bisect an angle of each of the three small triangles to determine the circle centres 1, 2, 3.

5. With radius 1B draw the three circles.

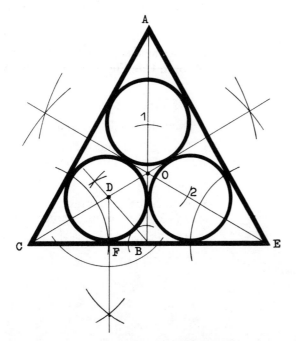

To Inscribe Three Equal Circles in an Equilateral Triangle, Each Circle to Touch Two Sides and Two Other Circles

1. Draw the given equilateral triangle.

2. Bisect two of the angles to determine the centre of the triangle, O.

3. Draw a line from A through O to B.

4. Bisect angle OBC to determine the centre of one of the circles, D.

5. With centre O and radius OD mark the centres of the other two circles, 1 and 2.

6. Draw DF perpendicular to CE from D.

7. With radius DF draw the three circles.

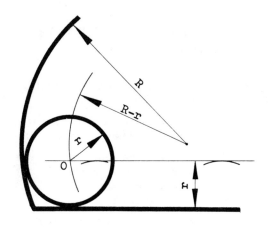

To Draw a Circle of Given Radius to Touch a Given Straight Line and an Arc as shown

1. Draw the given straight line, and given arc of radius R.

2. Draw a line parallel to the given straight line at a distance equal to the radius of the required circle, r.

3. With the centre of the given arc (R) as a centre and a radius of R–r, draw an arc to intersect the parallel line at O. This is the centre of required circle.

4. With centre O and radius r draw the required circle.

To Draw a Circle of Given Radius to Touch a Given Straight Line and an Arc as shown

1. Draw the given straight line, and the given arc of radius R.

2. Draw a line parallel to the given straight line at a distance equal to the radius of the required circle, r.

3. With the centre of the given arc as a centre and a radius of R+r, draw an arc to intersect the parallel line at O. This is the centre of the required circle.

4. With centre O and radius r draw the required circle.

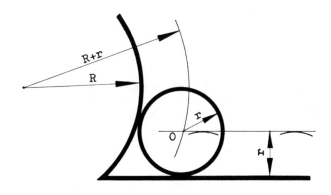

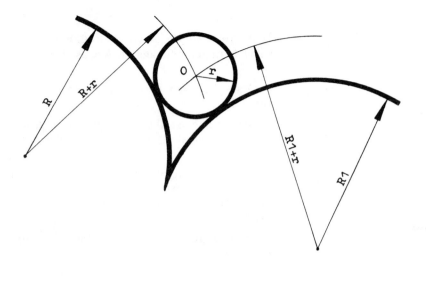

To Draw a Circle of Given Radius to Touch Two Given Arcs as shown

1. Draw the given arcs of radius R and R1. The radius of the given circle is r.

2. With the centre of the given arc of radius R as a centre and a radius R+r, draw an arc.

3. With the centre of the given arc of radius R1 as a centre and a radius R1+r, draw an arc to intersect the previous arc at O. This is the centre of the required circle.

4. With centre O and radius r draw the required circle.

To Draw a Circle of Given Radius to Touch Two Given Arcs as shown

1. Draw the given arcs of radius R and R1. The radius of the given circle is r.

2. With the centre of the given arc of radius R as a centre and a radius of R+r, draw an arc.

3. With the centre of the given arc of radius R1 as a centre and a radius R1−r, draw an arc to intersect the previous arc at O. This is the centre of the required circle.

4. With centre O and a radius r draw the required circle.

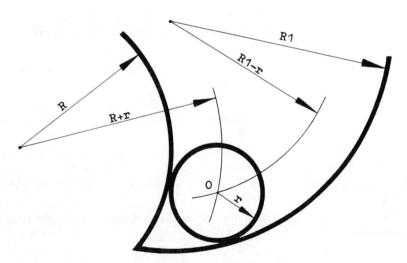

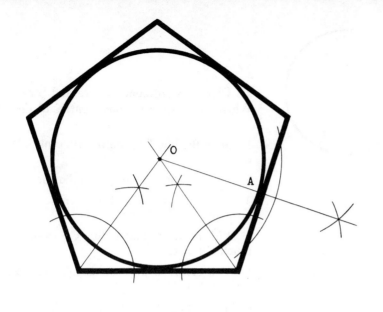

To Inscribe a Circle in any Regular Polygon, Rhombus or Deltoid

1. Bisect any two angles, to determine the centre of the figure, O

2. Draw a perpendicular to one side from the centre O (OA).

3. With centre O and radius OA draw the required circle.

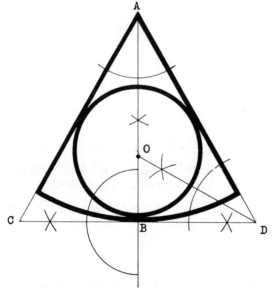

To Inscribe a Circle in any Sector

1. Bisect the angle (line AB).

3. Draw a tangent to meet the arms extended at C and D.

4. Bisect one of the angles to determine the centre of the required circle, O.

5. With centre O and radius OB draw the required circle.

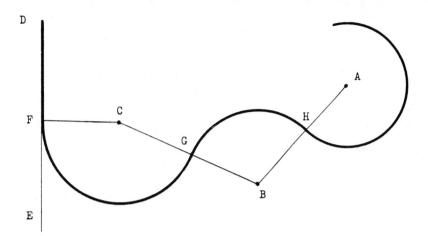

To Draw a Continuous Curve and Straight Line When Given the Line and Centres of the Arcs

1. Draw the line DE and the arc centres A, B and C.

2. Draw CF (a normal) perpendicular to DE.

3. Join CB and BA. These lines are common normals.

4. With centre C and radius CF draw an arc to touch CB at G.

5. With centre B and radius BG draw an arc to touch BA at H.

6. With centre A and radius AH draw an arc.

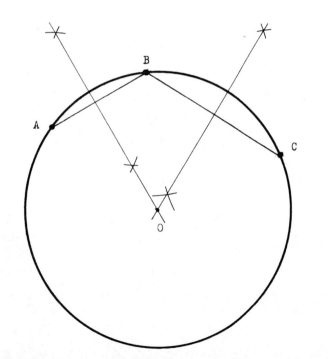

To Draw a Circle to Pass Through Three Given Points

1. Draw the given points A, B and C.

2. Bisect AB and BC. The bisectors intersect at O, the centre of the required circle.

3. With centre O and radius OC draw the circle.

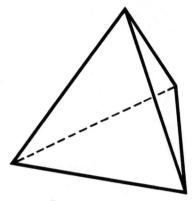

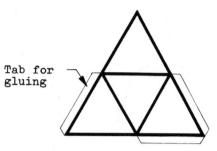

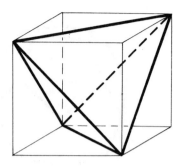

Tetrahedron

The tetrahedron is a regular solid bounded by 4 equilateral triangular faces.

Development of tetrahedron

Tab for gluing

Tetrahedron in a cube

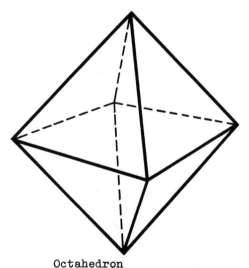

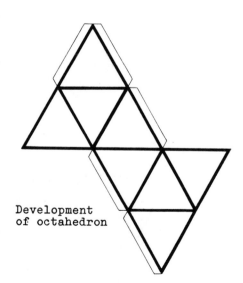

Development of octahedron

Octahedron

The octahedron is a regular solid bounded by 8 equilateral triangular faces.

Octahedron in a cube

45

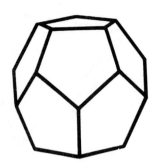

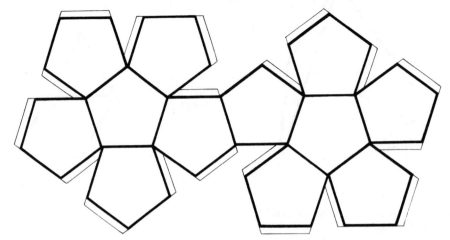

Dodecahedron

The dodecahedron is a regular solid bounded by 12 faces. Each face is a regular pentagon.

Development of dodecahedron

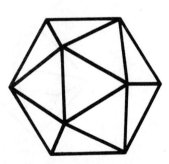

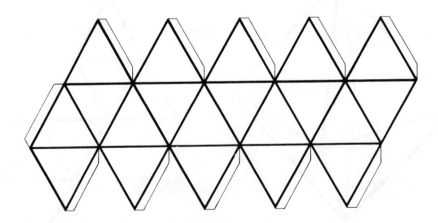

Icosahedron

The icosahedron is a regular solid bounded by 20 equilateral triangular faces.

Development of icosahedron

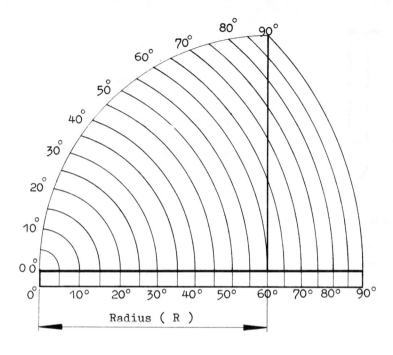

Radius (R)

To Draw a Scale of Chords to Show Distances of 5°

1. Draw any quadrant and divide the arc into 18 equal parts (first trisect the arc, and then divide each third into 3 equal parts with the dividers. There are now 9 equal parts. Divide each of these into 2 equal parts.)

2. Extend the base line of the quadrant to the right. With 00° as a centre, and a radius of 00°–5°, 00°–10°, etc. in turn, draw arcs to touch the base line of the quadrant and its extension.

3. Construct the scale beneath the quadrant. This scale is used to construct a required angle.

To Construct an Angle (say 25°) using the Scale of Chords

1. Draw a line AB.

2. With a radius of R (0°–60°) off the scale of chords and with centre A, draw an arc to cut line AB at C.

3. With a radius of 0°–25° off the scale of chords and with centre C, draw an arc to cut the previous arc at D.

4. Draw a line from A through D. DAB is the required angle.

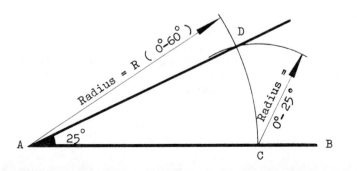

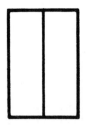

Triangular
Prism

Square
Prism

Hexagonal
Prism

PRISMS

A prism is named according to the shape of its base. Its edges are parallel to one another.

A line passing through the centre of each end is called the axis.

Triangular
Pyramid

Square
Pyramid

Hexagonal
Pyramid

PYRAMIDS

A pyramid is also named according to the shape of its base. It has sloping sides meeting at a point called the apex, which is vertically above the centre of the base. The axis passes through the centre of the base and the apex.

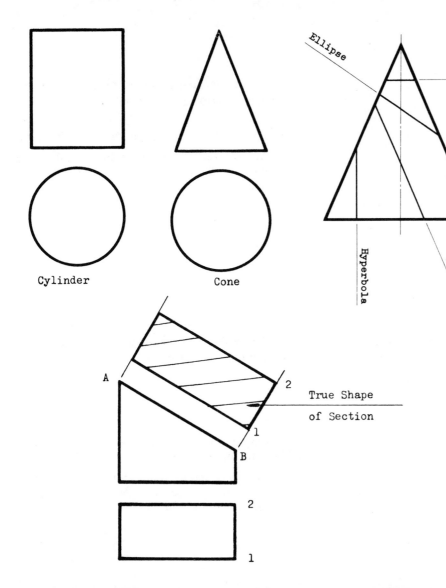

Cylinder

Cone

Ellipse

Circle

Conic Sections

Hyperbola

Parabola

A

B

2

1

True Shape

of Section

2

1

CONIC SECTIONS

The true shape of a section parallel to the slant side is a parabola. The true shape of a section parallel to the axis is a hyperbola. When a section is inclined to the axis and cutting both sides, its true shape is an ellipse. The true shape of a section at right angles to the axis is a circle.

SECTIONS

A rectangular prism is shown with its top sliced off. The sliced surface is called the section. An object that has had its top cut off is said to be truncated. The part remaining is called the frustum.

To Draw the True Shape of the Section

1. Draw lines perpendicular to the section from A and B. This is the true length of the section.

2. At any point draw line 1 parallel to the section.

3. Mark the true width of the section 1–2 from the plan.

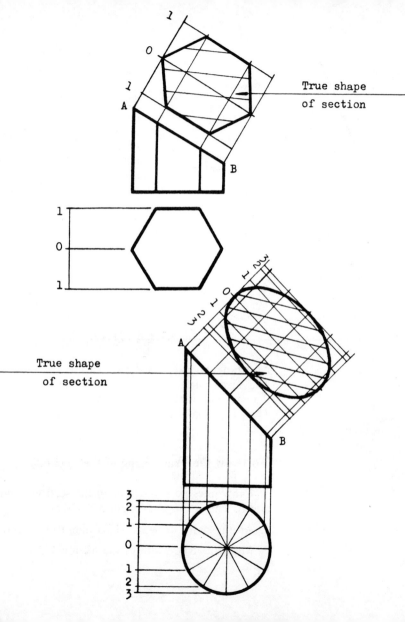

True shape
of section

To Draw the True Shape of the Section of the Truncated Hexagonal Prism

1. Project lines perpendicular to the section AB.

2. At any suitable point draw a centre line 0 parallel to the section. Mark 0–1 (obtained from the plan) each side of it.

To Draw the True Shape of the Section of the Frustum of the Cylinder

1. Divide the circumference of the plan into 12 equal parts. Project lines from these points to the section AB.

2. Project lines perpendicular to the section AB from the points on it.

3. At any suitable point draw a centre line 0 parallel to the section. Mark 0–1, 0–2, 0–3 (obtained from the plan) on each side of it.

True shape
of section

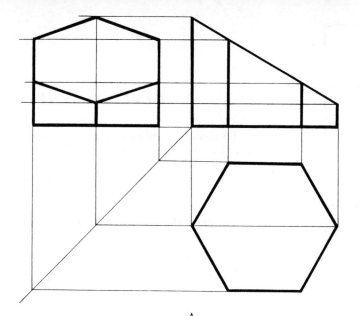

To Draw the End Elevation of the Frustum of the Hexagonal Prism

1. Project lines horizontally from each point on the front elevation as shown.

2. Transfer the plan widths vertically upwards.

3. Line in the end elevation.

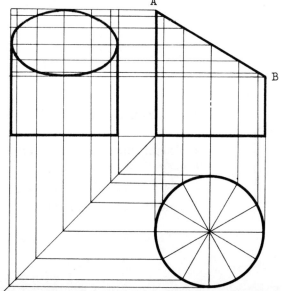

To Draw the End Elevation of the Frustum of the Cylinder

1. Divide the plan into 12 equal parts. Project these points vertically upwards to touch the section AB.

2. Project lines horizontally from each of the points on the front elevation as shown.

3. Transfer the plan widths vertically upwards.

4. Line in the end elevation.

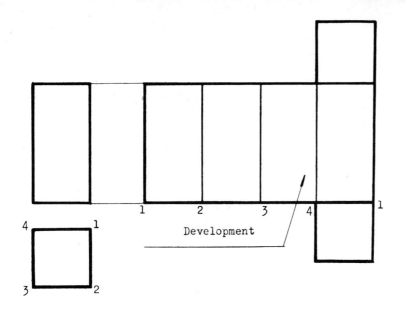

DEVELOPMENTS

To draw the development of an object means to draw the shape of all its surfaces laid out flat in one plane. The development when bent along certain lines will form the shape of the object.

To Draw the Development of the Square Prism

1. Project lines from the elevation to obtain the height of the sides.

2. Mark 1–2, 2–3, 3–4, 4–1 from the plan.

3. Add the top and bottom.

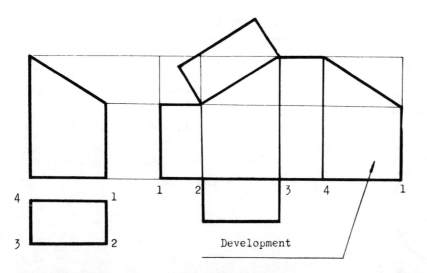

To Draw the Development of the Truncated Prism

1. Project lines from the elevation to obtain the heights of the sides.

2. Mark 1–2, 2–3, 3–4, 4–1 from the plan.

3. Add the top and bottom.

52

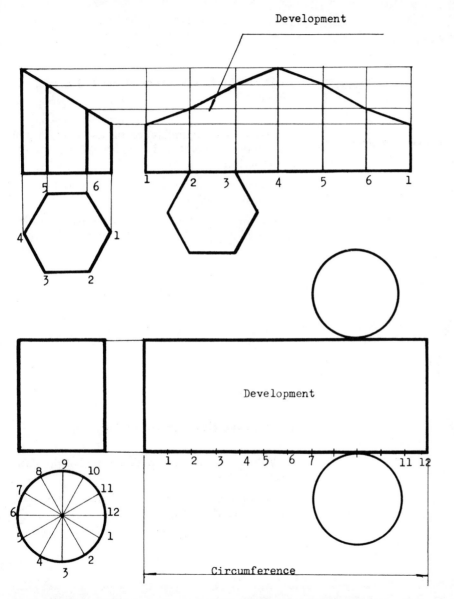

Development

To Draw the Development of the Frustum of the Hexagonal Prism

1. Project lines from the elevation to obtain the heights of the sides.

2. Mark 1–2, 2–3, 3–4, 4–5, 5–6, 6–1 from the plan.

To Draw the Development of the Cylinder

1. Divide the circumference of the plan into a number of equal parts, 1–12.

2. Project lines from the elevation to obtain the height of the side.

3. Mark units 1–12 from the plan (the circumference).

4. Add the top and bottom.

53

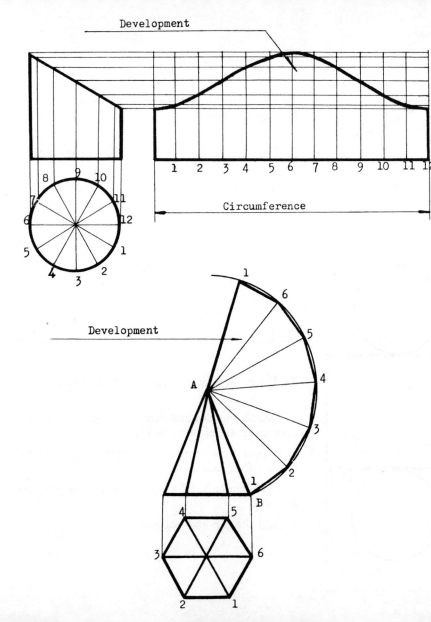

Development

Circumference

Development

To Draw the Development of the Frustum of the Cylinder

1. Divide the circumference of the plan into a number of equal parts 1–12 and project these points to the section.

2. Project lines from the elevation to obtain the heights of the curve.

3. Mark units 1–12. Draw lines from these to intersect the above projection lines to obtain the curve points.

To Draw the Development of a Pyramid

1. With apex A as a centre and radius of the slant height AB draw an arc.

2. Step off the chords 1–2, 2–3, 3–4, 4–5, 5–6, 6–1. Join these to the apex.

54

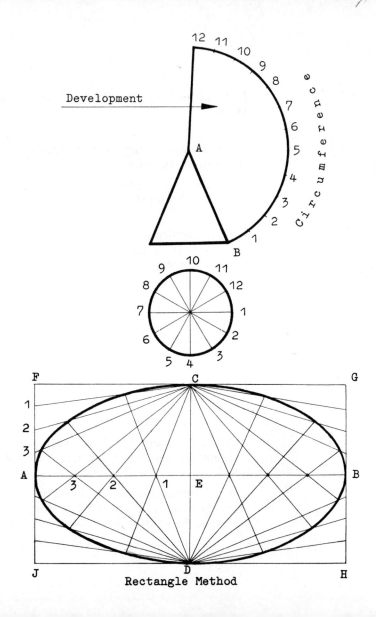

Development

Circumference

Rectangle Method

To Draw the Development of a Cone

1. With apex A as a centre and radius of the slant height AB draw an arc.

2. Divide the circumference of the base into a number of equal parts 1–12.

3. Step off units 1–12 along the arc. Join 12 to the apex.

THE ELLIPSE

The ellipse is a plane figure bounded by a curved line termed the circumference. Its longest diameter is called the major axis, its shortest diameter the minor axis. The two axes bisect at right angles.

To Draw an Ellipse by the Rectangle Method

1. Draw a rectangle equal to the major and minor axes. Draw the axes AB and CD.

2. Divide EA and AF into 4 equal units.

3. Radiate lines from C to 1, 2 and 3 on AF.

4. Radiate lines from D through 1, 2 and 3 on AE to intersect lines 1, 2 and 3. These are the curve points.

55

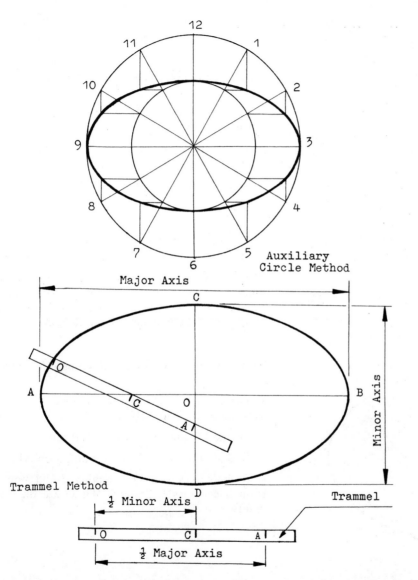

To Draw an Ellipse by the Auxiliary Circle Method

1. Draw two concentric circles equal in diameter to the major and minor axes.

2. Divide the circumference of the larger circle into 12 equal parts. Join these points to the centre of the circle.

3. Draw verticals from points 1–12 and draw horizontals from the points where the radiating lines cut the inner circle, to intersect the verticals. These are the curve points.

To Draw an Ellipse by the Trammel Method

1. Draw the two axes AB and CD.

2. Make a trammel by taking a strip of paper and marking half the major and minor axes as illustrated.

3. If the trammel is moved so that point C travels along the major axis and point A along the minor axis, then the point O will trace an ellipse.

56

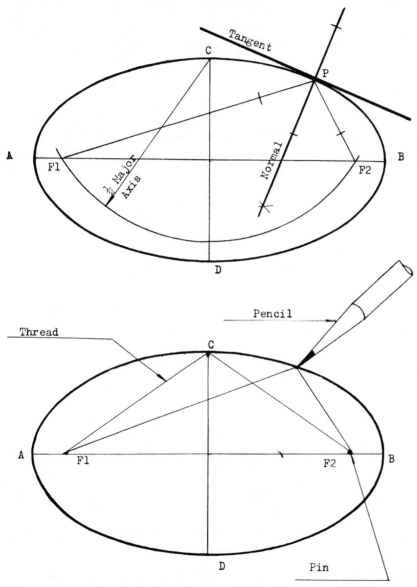

To Draw a Normal and a Tangent to an Ellipse at a Given Point on the Curve

1. With centre C and radius of half the major axis draw an arc to cut the major axis at F^1 and F^2. These are called the focal points.

2. Mark the given point P. Join P to F^1 and F^2.

3. Bisect angle F^1PF^2. The bisector is the required normal.

4. Draw a perpendicular to the normal from point P. This is the required tangent.

To Draw an Ellipse by the Foci Method

1. Draw the major and minor axes AB and CD and mark the focal points F^1 and F^2.

2. Place pins at F^1, F^2 and C and stretch a piece of thread taut.

3. Remove the pin at C and insert a pencil to trace the ellipse.

Foci Method

57

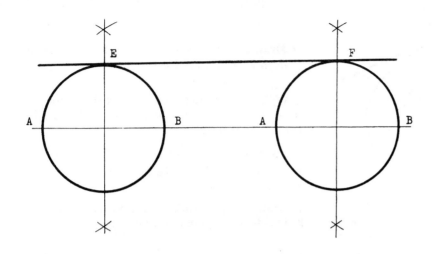

To Draw a Common External Tangent to Two Equal Circles

1. Draw a line through the centres of the circles.

2. Bisect the diameters AB. The bisectors cut the circumference of the circles at E and F.

3. Draw a line through E and F. This is the required tangent.

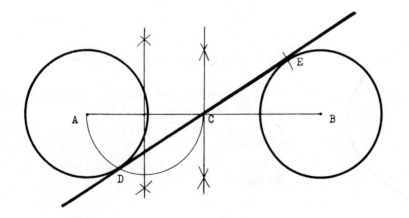

To Draw a Common Internal Tangent to Two Equal Circles

1. Join the centres A and B.

2. Bisect AB to give point C.

3. Construct a semicircle on AC cutting the circle at D.

4. With centre C and radius CD draw an arc cutting the second circle at E.

5. Draw a line through D and E. This is the required tangent.

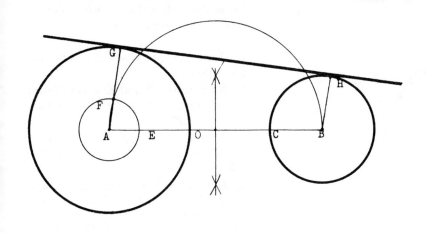

To Draw a Common External Tangent to Two Unequal Circles

1. Join the centres of the circles A and B.

2. Mark OE equal to CB.

3. With centre A and radius AE draw a circle.

4. Construct a semicircle on AB cutting the previous circle at F.

5. Draw a line from A through F cutting the circumference of the large circle at G.

6. Draw BH parallel to AG.

7. Draw a line through G and H. This is the required tangent.

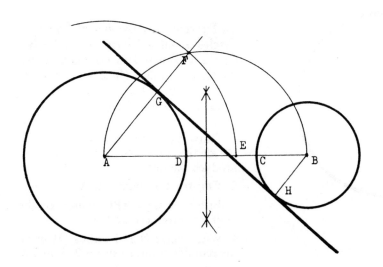

To Draw a Common Internal Tangent to Two Unequal Circles

1. Join the centres of the circles A and B.

2. Mark DE equal to CB.

3. With centre A and radius AE draw an arc.

4. Construct a semicircle on AB cutting the previous arc at F.

5. Draw line AF cutting the circumference of the large circle at G.

6. Draw BH parallel to AG.

7. Draw a line through G and H. This is the required tangent.

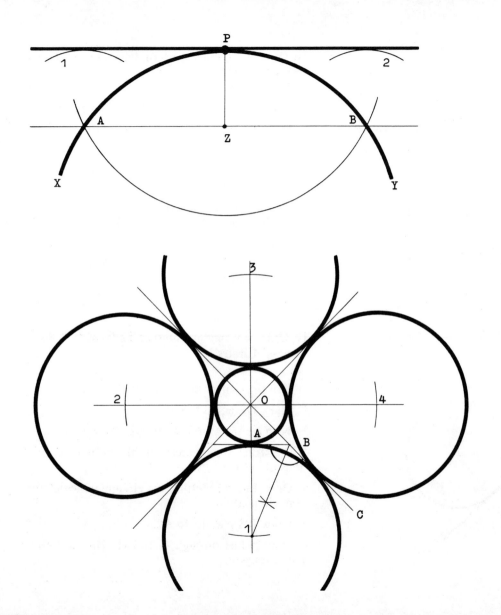

To Draw a Tangent at a Given Point on an Arc, when the Centre of the Arc is Not Given

1. Draw the given arc XY with the given point P.

2. With centre P and any convenient radius draw an arc to cut the given arc XY at A and B.

3. Draw a line through A and B. Draw a line perpendicular to this line from P (line PZ).

4. With A and B as centres in turn and radius PZ draw the arcs 1 and 2. Draw a line across these two arcs and through point P. This line is the required Tangent.

To Describe any number of Equal Circles about a Given Circle, Each Circle to Touch Two Others and also the Given Circles. (In this exercise we are to describe Four Equal Circles about the Given Circle)

1. Draw the given circle with centre O. Divide the circle into 8 equal parts, and produce the lines.

2. Construct a tangent at A.

3. Bisect the angle ABC to intersect the diameter produced at 1.

4. With centre O and radius O1 mark the remaining three centres 2, 3, and 4.

5. With radius A1 draw the required circles.

DIAGONAL SCALES

With a diagonal scale it is possible to measure to a fine degree of accuracy with 3 units of measurement, e.g. centimetres, millimetres and tenths of a millimetre.

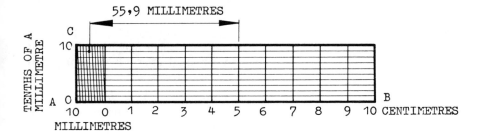

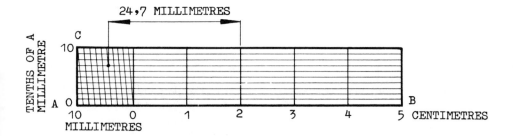

To Construct a Diagonal Scale of Centimetres to Read up to 11 Centimetres in Millimetres and Tenths of a Millimetre

1. Draw AB 11 centimetres long and divide it into 11 equal units.

2. Divide the first unit into 10 equal parts.

3. Erect a perpendicular AC (this can be any convenient height) and divide it into 10 equal parts. Draw horizontal lines from these units.

4. Transfer the 10 divisions of the first unit on AB to the top line and draw diagonals of one-unit slope as shown.

To Construct a Diagonal Scale of Twice Full Size to Read up to 6 Centimetres in Millimetres and Tenths of a Millimetre

1. Draw AB 12 centimetres long and divide it into 6 equal units.

2. Divide the first unit into 10 equal parts.

3. Erect a perpendicular AC (this can be any convenient height) and divide it into 10 equal parts. Draw horizontal lines from these units.

4. Transfer the 10 divisions of the first unit on AB to the top line and draw diagonals of one-unit slope as shown.

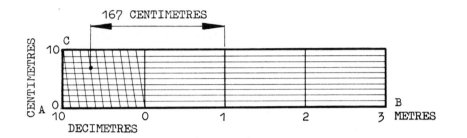

To Construct a Diagonal Scale of 3 Centimetres Equals 1 Metre to Read up to 4 Metres in Decimetres and Centimetres

1. Draw AB 12 centimetres long and divide it into 4 equal units.

2. Divide the first unit into 10 equal parts.

3. Erect a perpendicular AC (this can be any convenient height) and divide it into 10 equal units. Draw horizontal lines from these units.

4. Transfer the 10 divisions of the first unit on AB to the top line and draw diagonals of one-unit slope.

To Construct a Diagonal Scale of $\frac{1}{4}$ Full Size to Read up to 5 Decimetres in Centimetres and Millimetres

1. Draw AB 125 millimetres long ($\frac{1}{4}$ of 5 decimetres) and divide it into 5 equal units.

2. Divide the first unit into 10 equal parts.

3. Erect a perpendicular AC (this can be any convenient height) and divide it into 10 equal units. Draw horizontal lines from these units.

4. Transfer the 10 divisions of the first unit on AB to the top line and draw diagonals of one-unit slope as shown.

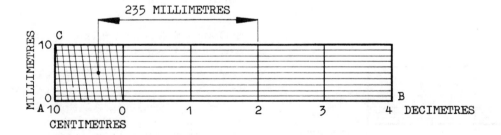

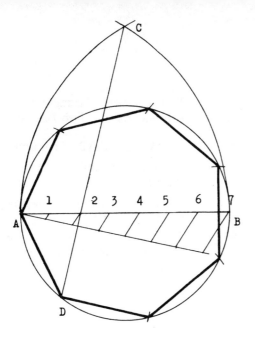

General Method of Constructing any Polygon in a Given Circle

1. Draw the given circle and divide the diameter AB into the same number of equal parts as the required polygon has sides.

2. With centres A and B in turn and radius AB draw arcs to intersect at C.

3. Draw a line from C through 2 to touch the circle at D. Line AD is one side of the polygon.

4. Step AD round the circle to obtain the remaining sides of the polygon.

To Draw any Polygon when Given the Diagonal

1. Draw a line AB any length and at any point C construct a semicircle of convenient radius and divide it into the same number of equal parts as the required polygon has sides.

2. Radiate lines from C through 2, 3 and 4. Draw CE and CF equal to the given diagonal.

3. Bisect CE and CF. The bisectors intersect at G.

4. With centre G and radius CG draw a circle. This will position the corners H and J.

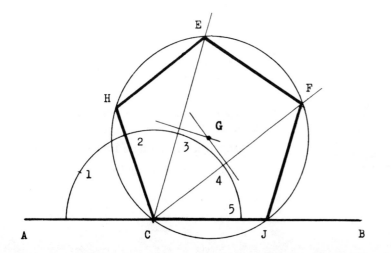

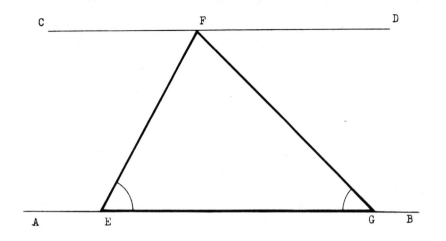

To Construct a Triangle when Given the Altitude and the Two Base Angles

1. Draw a line AB of convenient length.

2. Draw CD parallel to AB at a distance equal to the altitude.

3. Construct one of the base angles at E. The line touches CD at F.

4. Draw a line from F so that angle FGE is the other base angle. EFG is the required triangle.

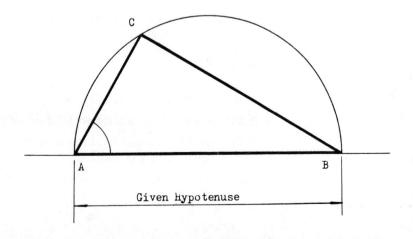

Given hypotenuse

To Construct a Triangle when Given the Hypotenuse and One Angle

1. Draw the hypotenuse AB and construct a semi-circle on it.

2. Draw the given angle BAC.

3. Join CB to complete the triangle.

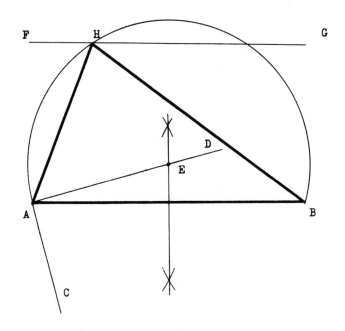

To Construct a Triangle when Given the Base, Altitude and Vertical Angle

1. Draw the base AB.

2. Draw AC so that angle BAC is equal to the vertical angle.

3. Draw AD perpendicular to AC.

4. Bisect AB. The bisector cuts AD at E.

5. With centre E and radius AE draw a circle.

6. Draw FG parallel to AB at a distance equal to the altitude, to cut the circle at H.

7. Join AH and HB.

To Construct an Isosceles Triangle when Given the Perimeter and Vertical Height

1. Draw a line AB equal to the perimeter.

2. Bisect AB at C and erect a perpendicular CD equal to the vertical height.

3. Join AD and DB.

4. Construct angles ADE and BDF at D equal to the base angles A and B.

5. EDF is the isosceles triangle.

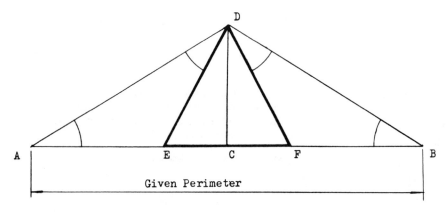

Given Perimeter

65

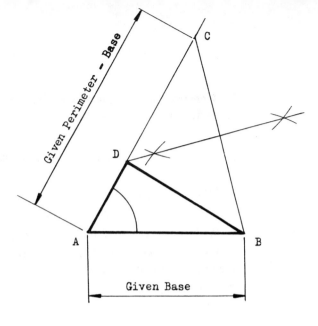

To Construct a Triangle Given the Base, One Base Angle and the Perimeter

1. Draw the base AB.

2. Construct the given angle at A and mark off AC, which is the perimeter minus base AB.

3. Join C to B and bisect it. The bisector cuts AC at D.

4. ADB is the required triangle.

To Construct a Triangle when Given the Altitude, the Perimeter and the Angle at the Vertex

1. Draw AB and AC so that angle BAC is equal to the angle at the vertex.

2. Mark AD equal to half the perimeter. Mark AE equal to half the perimeter.

3. Draw perpendiculars at D and E to intersect at F.

4. With centre F and radius DF draw an arc. With centre A and radius equal to the altitude draw a second arc. Draw a common tangent to the two arcs to give points G and H.

5. AGH is the required triangle.

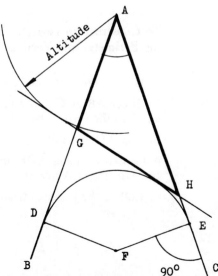

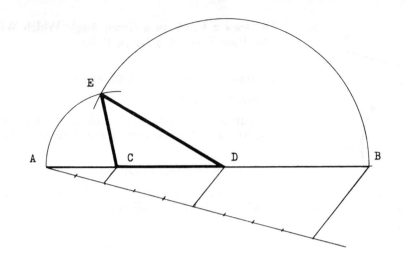

To Construct a Triangle Given the Perimeter and the Sides in a Given Ratio

1. Draw a line AB equal to the perimeter.

2. Divide AB in the given ratio by proportional division (in the example shown 2:3:4).

3. With centre C and radius CA draw an arc. With centre D and radius DB draw an arc to cut the previous one at E.

4. CED is the required triangle.

To Construct a Triangle Similar to a Given Triangle but with a Different Perimeter

1. Draw the given triangle ABC and extend AC.

2. With centre A and radius AB draw an arc to cut AC extended at D.

3. With centre C and radius CB draw an arc to cut AC extended at E.

4. Draw DF equal to the perimeter of the required triangle, at any convenient angle.

5. Draw CG and AH parallel to EF.

6. With centre H and radius HD draw an arc. With centre G and radius GF draw an arc to cut the previous one at J.

7. HJG is the required triangle.

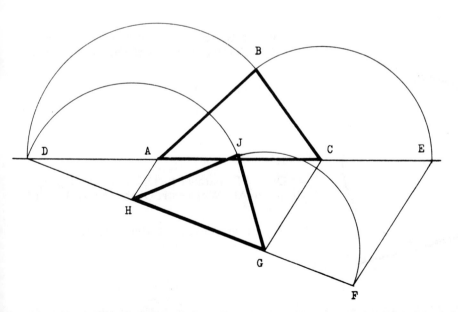

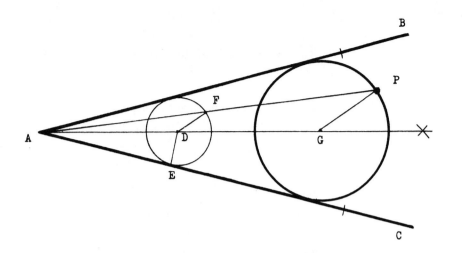

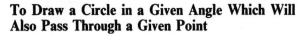

To Draw a Circle in a Given Angle Which Will Also Pass Through a Given Point

1. Draw the given angle BAC and point P.

2. Bisect angle BAC.

3. With any centre D, draw a circle touching AB and AC. Join P to A, cutting the circle at F. Join DF.

4. Draw PG parallel to DF.

5. With centre G and radius GP, draw a circle which will also touch AB and AC.

To Draw a Series of Circles in a Given Angle to Touch Each Other and Also the Sides of the Angle

1. Bisect angle BAC.

2. Draw a perpendicular to AC from E to give point O. With centre O and radius OE draw a circle.

3. Join ED.

4. Draw FE^1 parallel to DE. Draw E^{1}O^1 perpendicular to AC. With centre O^1 and radius O^{1}E^1 draw a circle.

5. Repeat the above for further circles.

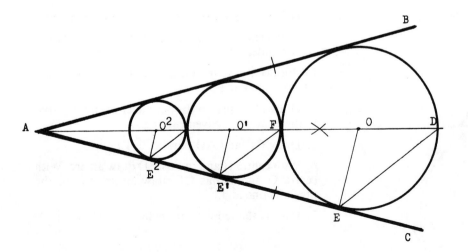

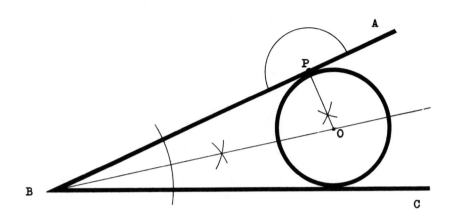

To Draw a Circle Tangential to Two Converging Lines and Touching One of them at a Given Point

1. Draw the given angle ABC and the given point P.

2. Bisect the angle.

3. Draw a line perpendicular to AB from P to intersect the bisector of the angle at O

6. With centre O and radius PO draw the required circle.

To Draw a Circle to Touch a Given Circle and also a Given Line at a Given Point

1. Draw the given circle with centre O and the given line AB with the given point P.

2. Draw a line perpendicular to AB from P (line PC).

3. Draw a line perpendicular to AB through the centre of the circle, O (line ED).

4. Draw line EP. F is the point where this line cuts the circumference of the given circle.

5. Draw a line from O through F to touch the perpendicular PC at G.

6. With centre G and radius GP draw the required circle.

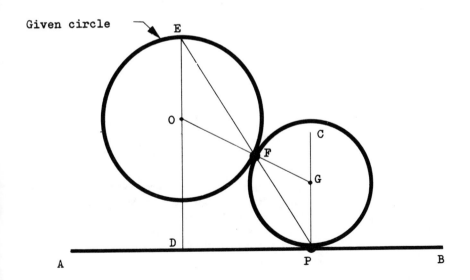

Given circle

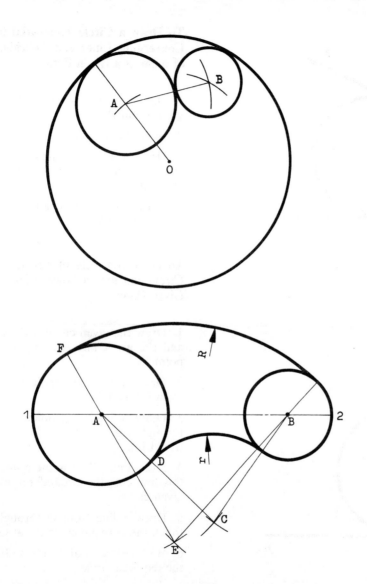

To Draw Two Circles Within a Given Circle When Given their Radii. The Circles to Touch Each Other

1. Draw the given large circle (radius R) with centre O.

2. Draw one of the other two given circles (radius r) of centre A.

3. With centre O and radius R—radius of third circle, draw an arc.

4. With centre A and a radius of r+radius of third circle, draw an arc to cut the previous one at B, the centre of the third circle.

To Draw an Internal and an External Arc of Given Radii to Touch Two Given Circles

1. Draw the two given circles of radius A1 and B2.

2. Let the internal arc radius be r and the external radius R.

3. To draw the internal arc. With centre A and radius r+A1 draw an arc. With centre B and radius r+B2 draw an arc to cut the previous one at C. Join C to A and B. With centre C and radius CD draw the arc.

4. To draw the external arc. With centre A and radius R—A1 draw an arc. With centre B and radius R—B2 draw an arc to cut the previous one at E. Draw a line from E through A to F and a line from E through B. With centre E and radius EF draw the arc.

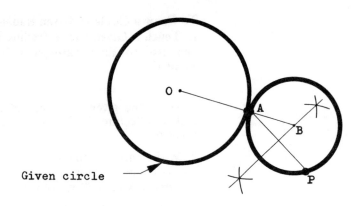

Given circle

To Draw a Circle to Pass Through a Given Point (P) and also Touch a Given Circle at a Given Point (A)

1. Draw the given circle with centre O and the given point A. Draw the given point P.

2. Join AP and bisect this line.

3. Draw a line from O through A to intersect the bisector of AP at B. This is the centre of the required circle.

4. With centre B and radius BA draw the required circle; which will also pass through the point P.

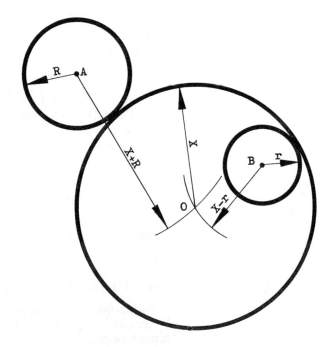

To Draw a Circle of Given Radius to Touch Two Given Circles of Given Centres. The Circle is to Include One Circle and Exclude the Other

1. Draw the two given circles of radius R and radius r and their centres A and B. The radius of the required circle is X.

2. With centre A and radius X+R describe an arc.

3. With centre B and radius X−r describe an arc to cut the previous arc at O. This is the centre of the required circle.

4. With centre O and radius X draw the required circle.

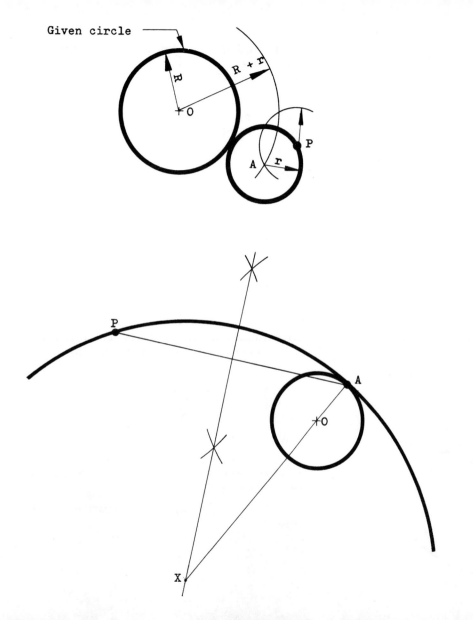

Given circle

To Draw a Circle of Given Radius (r) to Touch a Given Circle (radius R) and also to Pass Through a Given Point (P)

1. Draw the given circle of radius R and with centre O. Draw the given point P.

2. With centre O, and a radius of the given circle + the radius of the required circle, R + r, draw an arc.

3. With centre P and the radius of the required circle, r, draw an arc to intersect the previous arc at A.

4. With centre A and radius r, draw the required circle.

To Draw a Circle to Pass Through a Given Point (P) and Touch a Given Circle at a Given Point (A) and also Enclosing the Circle

1. Draw the given point P, and the given circle of centre O with the given point A.

2. Join PA, and bisect this line.

3. Draw a line from A through O to intersect the bisector at X. This is the centre of the required circle.

4. With centre X and radius XA, draw the required circle. This will also pass through point P.

72

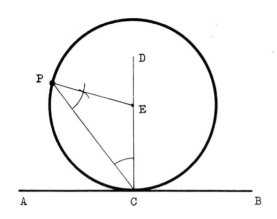

To Draw a Circle to Pass Through a Given Point and Touch a Line at a Given Point

1. Draw the given point P and the given point C on the line AB.

2. Draw CD perpendicular to AB.

3. Join CP and at P make an angle CPE equal to angle PCD. E is the centre of the required circle.

To Draw a Circle to Pass Through Two Given Points and Touch a Given Line

1. Draw the two given points A and B and the given line CD.

2. Extend a line from A through B.

3. Extend CD to touch AB extended at E.

4. Mark EF equal to EB.

5. Construct a semicircle on AF.

6. Draw a line perpendicular to AF from E to touch the semicircle at G.

7. Mark EH equal to EG.

8. Draw a line perpendicular to CD at H. Bisect AB to cut the previous line at J, the centre of the required circle.

9. With centre J and radius JH draw the circle.

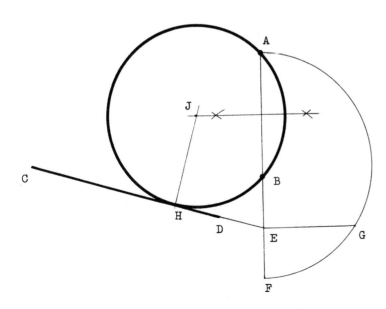

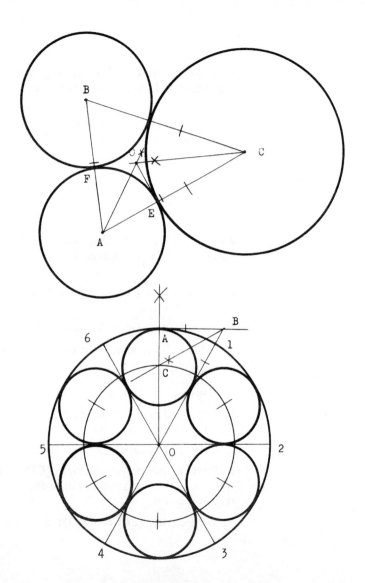

To Draw Three Circles Touching Each Other when Given the Position of Their Centres

1. Draw the three given centres A, B and C and connect them. Find the centre O of the triangle formed.

2. Draw a perpendicular to any side from O (OE).

3. With centre A and radius AE draw a circle.

4. With centre C and radius CE draw the second circle.

5. With centre B and radius BF draw the third circle.

To Draw any Number of Equal Circles in a Given Circle

1. Draw the given circle and divide the circumference into the same number of equal parts as the required number of circles to be drawn in it. Join each division to the centre O.

2. Bisect one sector. The bisector cuts the circumference at A. Draw a line at right angles to OA and extend OI to cut it at B.

3. Bisect angle ABO. The bisector cuts OA at C. With centre O and radius OC draw a circle and bisect each sector to intersect this to locate the circle centres.

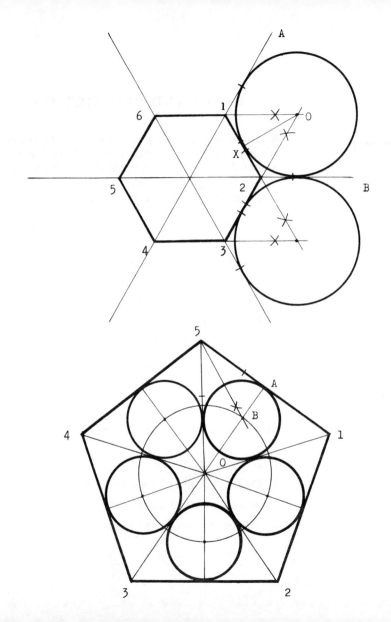

To Draw Equal Circles Around a Regular Polygon to Touch Each Other and One Side of the Polygon

1. Radiate lines from the centre of the polygon through each corner.

2. Bisect angle A12 and angle B21. The bisectors intersect at O, the centre of the circle.

3. Draw a perpendicular to 12 from O (OX).

4. With centre O and radius OX draw a circle.

5. Repeat the above procedure for each circle.

To Draw a Number of Equal Circles in a Regular Polygon to Touch Each Other and One Side of the Polygon

1. Radiate lines from the centre of the polygon to each corner.

2. Bisect each side.

3. Bisect angle O51. The bisector cuts OA at B. With centre O and radius OB draw a circle to locate the circle centres.

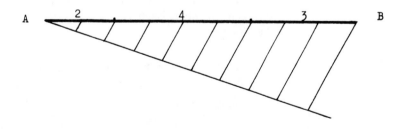

RATIO AND PROPORTION

A ratio is a relationship between numbers or lines. We may compare two numbers and say 2 is to 4, written 2:4. This is the ratio of these two numbers.

In proportion we have two equal ratios. For example we may say 1:2 as 2:4, written 1:2::2:4.

To Divide a Given Line in a Ratio 3:2

1. Draw the given line AB.
2. Divide AB into (3+2=5) 5 equal parts.
3. Mark 3 and 2 units.
4. The line is now in the ratio 3:2.

To Divide a Given Line in a Ratio 2:4:3

1. Draw the given line AB.
2. Divide AB into (2+4+3=9) 9 equal parts.
3. Mark 2, 4 and 3 units.
4. The line is now in the ratio 2:4:3.

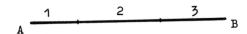

To Draw the Line CD in the Same Proportion as AB

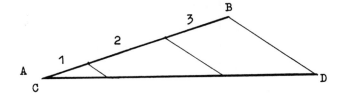

1. Draw CD and at any convenient angle draw a line from C and on it mark AB and the dimensions 1, 2 and 3.

2. Join BD and draw lines parallel to it from the divisions. CD is now divided in the same proportion as AB.

To Draw a Similar Figure to ABCDE, Enlarged so that AB is 60 Millimetres Long

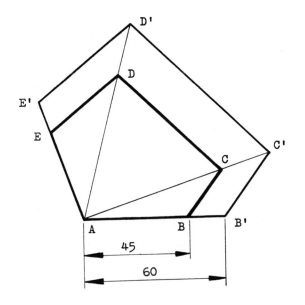

1. Draw the polygon. Make AB 45 millimetres.

2. Draw AB' 60 millimetres long as required.

3. Radiate lines from A through the corners C, D and E.

4. Draw B'C' parallel to BC.

5. Draw C'D' parallel to CD.

6. Draw D'E' parallel to DE to complete the enlarged figure.

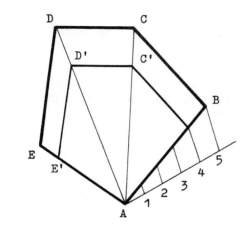

To Draw a Polygon Similar to Another with its Sides Reduced in a Given Ratio

1. Let the polygon be ABCDE and the ratio 5:4.
2. Divide AB into 5 equal parts.
3. Radiate lines from A to the corners C and D.
4. Draw unit 4C′ parallel to BC.
5. Draw C′D′ parallel to CD.
6. Draw D′E′ parallel to DE to complete the reduced figure.

To Draw a Figure Similar to Another with the Sides Reduced in a Given Ratio

1. Let the figure be ABCD and the ratio 5:3.
2. Mark point P any convenient distance from the figure.
3. Radiate lines from P to A, B, C, D.
4. Divide PA into 5 equal parts.
5. Draw a line A′D′ from unit 3 (A1) parallel to AD.
6. Draw D′C′ parallel to DC.
7. Draw C′B′ parallel to CB.
8. Draw B′A′ parallel to BA, to complete the reduced figure.

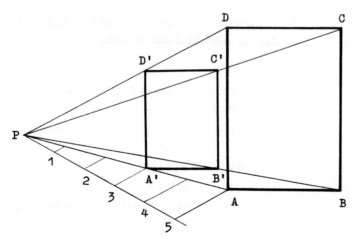

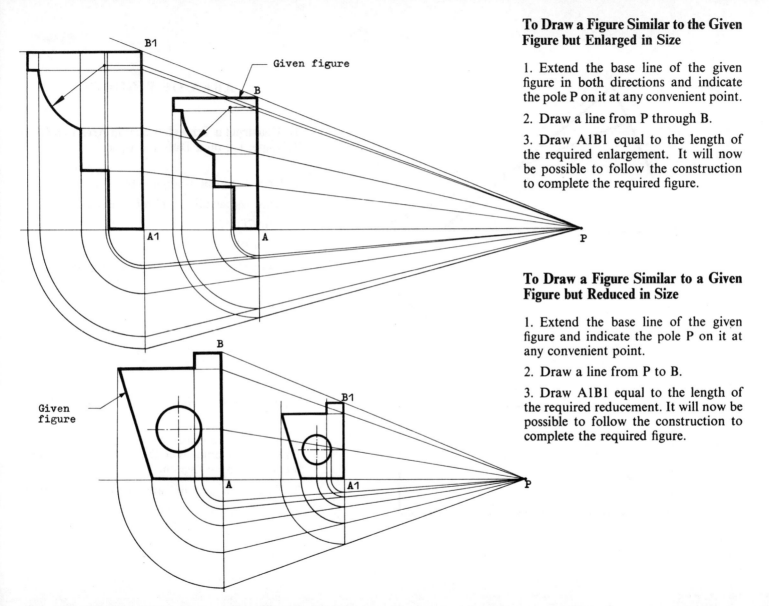

To Draw a Figure Similar to the Given Figure but Enlarged in Size

1. Extend the base line of the given figure in both directions and indicate the pole P on it at any convenient point.

2. Draw a line from P through B.

3. Draw A1B1 equal to the length of the required enlargement. It will now be possible to follow the construction to complete the required figure.

To Draw a Figure Similar to a Given Figure but Reduced in Size

1. Extend the base line of the given figure and indicate the pole P on it at any convenient point.

2. Draw a line from P to B.

3. Draw A1B1 equal to the length of the required reducement. It will now be possible to follow the construction to complete the required figure.

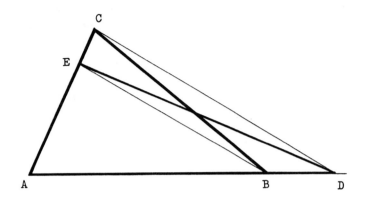

AREA OF FIGURES

To Construct a Triangle Equal in Area to a Given Triangle, but on a Different Base

1. Draw the given triangle ABC.

2. Draw the required different base AD.

3. Join CD.

4. Draw BE parallel to DC.

5. Join ED. AED is the required triangle.

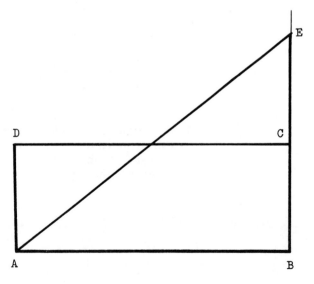

To Construct a Triangle when Given the Area

1. Let the given area be $4\frac{1}{2}$ square centimetres. Draw any rectangle ABCD equal to the given area. $3 \text{ cm} \times 1\frac{1}{2} \text{ cm} = 4\frac{1}{2}$ sq. cm.

2. Extend one side, BC, and mark CE equal to BC.

3. Join EA. ABE is the required triangle.

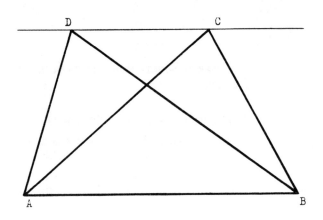

Triangles on the Same Base and Between Parallels have Equal Areas

Triangles ABC and ABD have equal area.

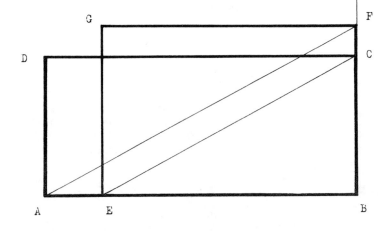

To Construct a Rectangle of Different Side but Equal in Area to a Given Rectangle

1. Draw the given rectangle ABCD.
2. Mark EB equal to the required different side.
3. Draw CE.
4. Extend BC and draw AF parallel to EC.
5. EBFG is the required rectangle.

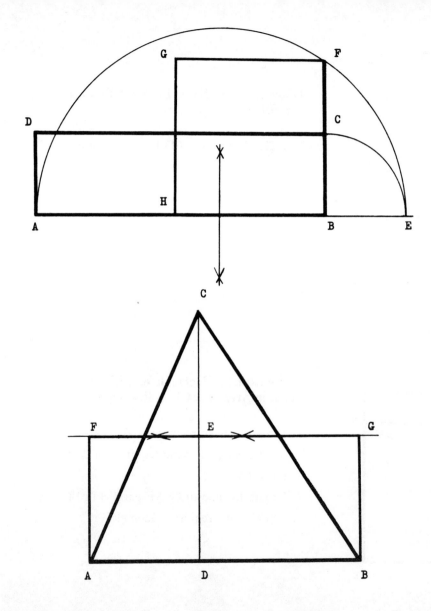

To Draw a Square Equal in Area to a Given Rectangle

1. Draw the given rectangle ABCD.

2. Extend AB at B. With centre B and radius BC draw an arc to touch AB extended at E.

3. Erect a semicircle on AE. Extend BC to touch it at F. BF is the length of side of the square.

To Draw a Rectangle Equal in Area to a Given Triangle

1. Draw the given triangle ABC.

2. Draw a perpendicular to AB from C to give point D.

3. Bisect CD to give E.

4. Draw a parallel line to AB through E. Draw perpendiculars at A and B to give points F and G. ABGF is the required rectangle.

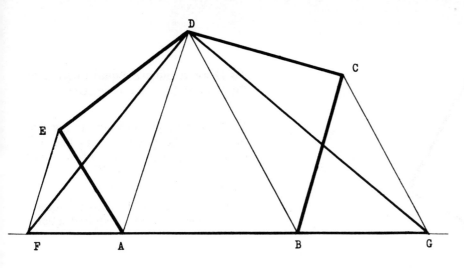

To Construct a Triangle Equal in Area to a Given Polygon

1. Draw the given polygon ABCDE.
2. Extend AB at both ends.
3. Join AD and BD.
4. Draw EF parallel to AD and CG parallel to BD.
5. Join FD and GD. FDG is the required triangle.

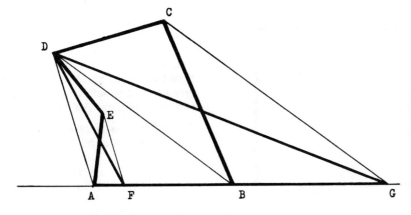

To Construct a Triangle Equal in Area to a Given Polygon with an External Angle

1. Draw the given polygon ABCDE.
2. Join DA and draw EF parallel to it. Join DF.
3. Join DB and draw CG parallel to it. Join DG.
4. FDG is the required triangle.

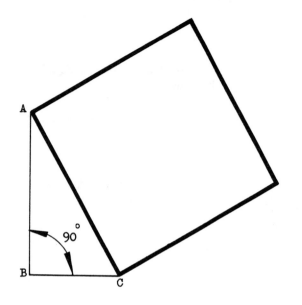

To Draw a Square Equal in Area to the Sum of Two Given Squares

1. Draw AB equal in length to the side of one of the given squares and BC equal in length to the side of the other given square. AB and BC are drawn perpendicular to each other.

2. Join A to C and construct a square on this line. This is the required square.

To Draw a Square Equal in Area to the Difference of Two Given Squares

1. Draw AB equal in length to the side of the given smaller square. Construct a perpendicular (AX) at A. With centre B and a radius equal to the side of the given larger square draw an arc to cut the perpendicular AX at C.

2. Construct a square on AC. This is the required square.

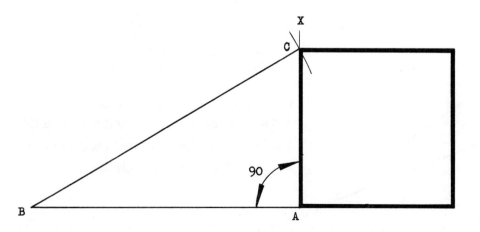

To Draw a Triangle Equal in Area to a Given Parallelogram

1. Draw the given parallelogram ABCD.

2. Join A to C.

3. Extend base line BA. Draw DE parallel to AC from D.

4. Join E to C. EBC is the required triangle.

To Draw a Triangle Equal in Area to any Regular Polygon

1. Draw the regular polygon—in this exercise a hexagon is shown.

2. Draw the diagonals to intersect at the centre of the polygon, O.

3. Draw AB equal in length to length of side × number of sides—in this exercise AB is equal to six times the length of the side of the hexagon.

4. Join O to A and O to B. ABO is the required triangle.

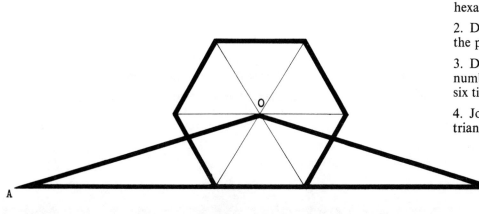

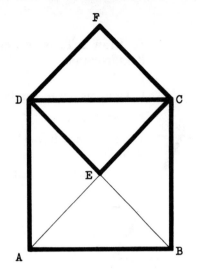

To Draw a Square having Half the Area of a Given Square

1. Draw the given square ABCD.

2. Draw the diagonals AC and BD. The diagonals intersect at E.

3. Draw the required square DECF.

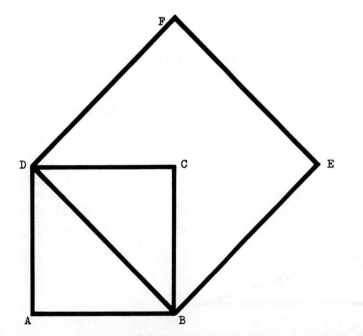

To Draw a Square having Twice the Area of a Given Square

1. Draw the given square ABCD.

2. Draw the diagonal BD, which is the length of side of the required square. Construct the square on the diagonal BD. BEFD is the required square.

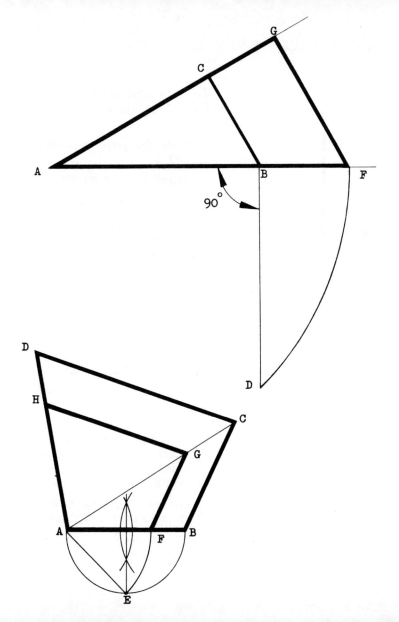

To Draw a Plane Figure Similar to a Given Figure, but Twice its Area

1. Draw the given figure ABC.

2. Draw BD perpendicular to AB and the same length as AB.

3. Extend AC and AB.

4. With centre A and radius AD draw an arc to cut AB extended at F.

5. Draw FG parallel to BC. AFG is the required figure.

To Draw a Plane Figure Similar to a Given Figure, but Half its Area

1. Draw the given figure ABCD.

2. Bisect AB and draw a semicircle on AB. The bisector cuts the semicircle at E.

3. With centre A and radius AE draw an arc to cut AB at F.

4. Draw AC. Draw FG parallel to BC and GH parallel to CD. The required figure is AFGH.

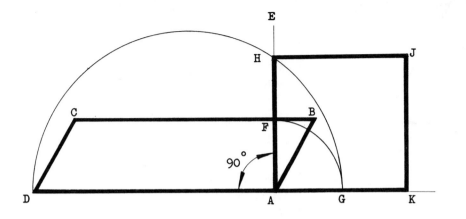

To Draw a Square Equal in Area to a Given Parallelogram

1. Draw the given parallelogram ABCD.

2. Extend DA to the right.

3. Construct a perpendicular at A (AE).

4. With centre A and radius AF draw an arc to cut the extension of DA at G.

5. Construct a semicircle on DG.

6. The perpendicular AE cuts the semi-circle at H. AH is length of the required square.

To Draw a Circle Equal in Area to the Sum of Two Given Circles

1. Draw AB equal in diameter to one of the given circles and BC equal in diameter to the other given circle. The two lines are to be perpendicular to each other.

2. Draw a line from C to A. CA is the diameter of the required circle.

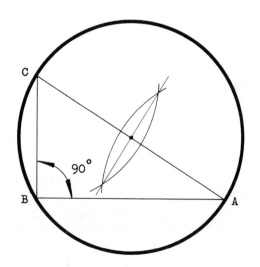

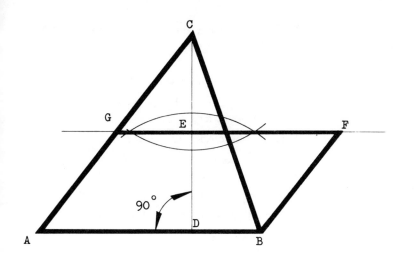

To Draw a Parallelogram Equal in Area to a Given Triangle

1. Draw the given triangle ABC.

2. Draw a perpendicular, CD, to the base AB from the apex C. Bisect CD and extend the bisector to the left and to the right of E. Draw BF parallel to AG. ABFG is the required parallelogram.

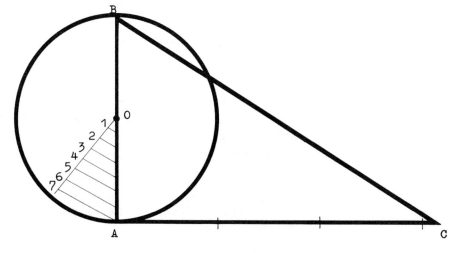

To Draw a Triangle Equal in Area to a Given Circle

1. Draw the given circle of diameter AB and centre O.

2. Divide the radius OA into 7 equal parts.

3. Draw AC perpendicular to AB and $3\frac{1}{7}$ times OA.

4. Join C to B. ACB is the required triangle.

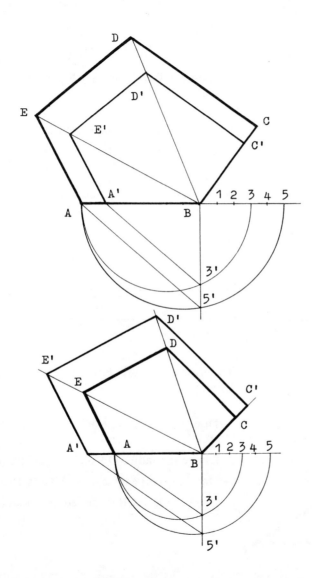

To Draw a Similar Polygon, of Ratio 3:5 in Area, to a Given Polygon

1. Draw the given polygon ABCDE.

2. Extend AB from B and mark 5 equal units of any convenient length.

3. Draw semicircles on A3 and A5.

4. Draw a perpendicular to AB from B to cut the semicircles at 3' and 5'.

5. Join A5' and draw 3'A' parallel to it.

6. Radiate lines from B to E and D.

7. Draw A'E' parallel to AE. Draw E'D' parallel to ED. Draw D'C' parallel to DC to complete the required polygon.

To Draw a Similar Polygon, of Ratio 5:3 in Area, to a Given Polygon

1. Draw the given polygon ABCDE.

2. Extend AB in both directions and mark 5 equal units of any convenient length from B.

3. Draw semicircles on A3 and A5.

4. Draw a perpendicular to AB from B to cut the semicircles at 3'5'.

5. Join A3' and draw 5'A' parallel to it.

6. Radiate lines from B through E and D.

7. Draw A'E' parallel to AE. Draw E'D' parallel to ED. Draw D'C' parallel to DC to complete the required polygon.

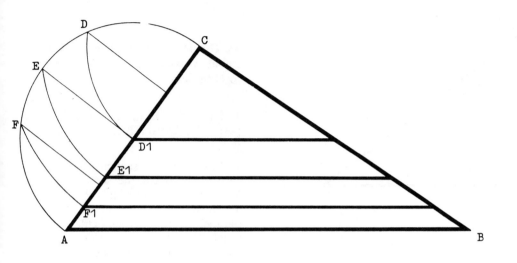

To Divide any Triangle into a Given Number of Equal Areas (4 in this exercise) by Lines Drawn Parallel to One Side

1. Draw the given triangle ABC. Construct a semicircle on AC. Divide AC into 4 equal parts and draw perpendiculars to AC from these points to touch the semicircle at D, E, F.

2. With centre C, and radius CD, CE and CF in turn, draw arcs to touch AC at D1, E1, F1. Draw lines from these points parallel to AB. The triangle is now divided into 4 equal areas.

To Divide a Rectangle or Parallelogram into Two Equal Areas from Any Point (P) on One of its Sides

1. Draw the rectangle or parallelogram ABCD and the given point P.

2. Draw diagonals AC and BD to intersect at E. Draw a line from P through E to touch AB. This line divides the figure into 2 equal areas.

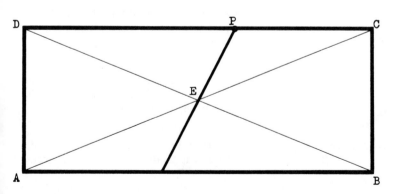

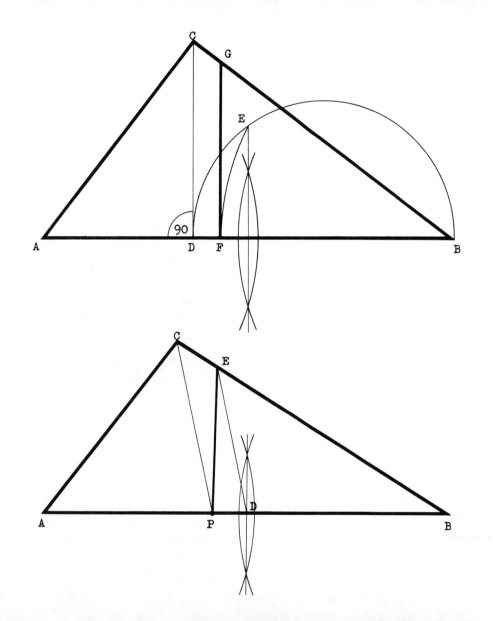

To Divide any Triangle into Two Equal Areas by a Line Perpendicular to One Side

1. Draw the triangle ABC. Draw a perpendicular to AB from the vertex C (CD).

2. Construct a semicircle on DB. Bisect AB to cut the semicircle at E. With centre B and radius BE, draw an arc to cut AB at F. Draw a line from F parallel to the perpendicular CD to touch BC at G. The line FG divides the triangle into two equal areas.

To Divide any Triangle into Two Equal Areas by a Line Drawn from a Given Point on One of its Sides

1. Draw the triangle ABC with the given point P. Draw a line from the given point P to the vertex C.

2. Bisect AB to obtain point D. Draw DE from D parallel to PC. Line PE divides the triangle into 2 equal areas.

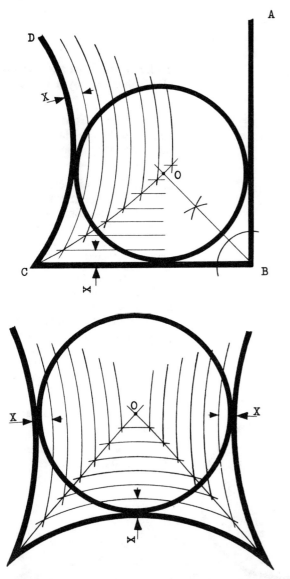

To Draw a Circle to Touch Two Given Straight Lines and a Given Arc as shown

1. Draw the given lines AB and BC and the given arc CD.

2. Take any convenient unit, X, and draw lines at this distance and parallel to line BC and arc CD to intersect as shown. Draw a curve through the intersections.

3. Bisect angle ABC. The bisector cuts the curve at O. This is the centre of the required circle.

4. Draw a perpendicular to one of the straight lines from O (not shown for clarity) to obtain the radius of the required circle, and with centre O draw the circle.

To Draw a Circle to Touch Three Given Arcs as shown

1. Draw the three given arcs.

2. Take any convenient unit, X, and draw arcs at this distance and parallel to the given arcs to intersect as shown. Draw the curves through the intersections. The curves intersect at O. This is the centre of the required circle.

3. Draw a normal to one of the given arcs (not shown for clarity) from O to obtain the radius of the required circle, and with centre O draw the circle.

To Draw the Plan and the True Shape of a Sphere cut by a Plane as shown

1. Draw the front elevation of the sphere cut by the plane A–A inclined to the horizontal plane, and the outline of the plan.

2. Draw a semicircle on the section. BB, and divide it into 6 equal parts. Project these points, perpendicular to the section, to touch the section. From the points on the section project vertical lines downwards.

3. Take the widths O–1X, O–2X, O–3X, and place these each side of the centre line on the plan. Draw these points horizontally to intersect the vertical projections from the section. The intersections of the lines gives the points for the curve of the plan of the section.

4. To obtain the circle which is the true shape of the section, take half of the section BB as a radius and draw the circle.

Every cut on a sphere will have a circle for its true shape.

True shape of section is a circle

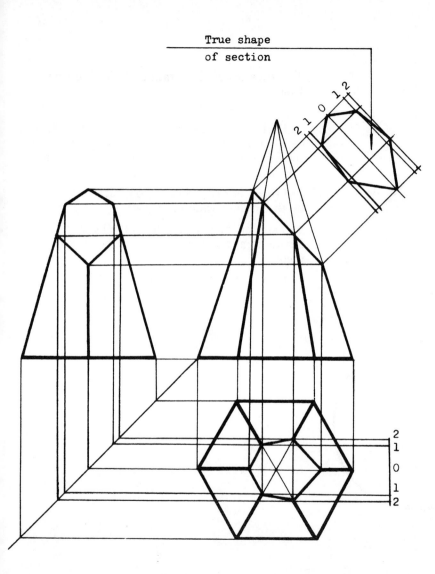

True shape
of section

To Draw the End Elevation and the True Shape of the Section of a Frustum of a Pyramid

1. Draw the elevation and plan of the frustum.

2. Project vertical lines from the edges on the section to cut the edges on the plan. Draw the plan of the section. Mark the plan widths of the section O1, O2.

3. Draw lines perpendicular to the section from the edge points on it.

4. Draw centre line O parallel to the section at any convenient distance from it. Mark the plan widths O1, O2 each side of it. Draw the true shape of the section.

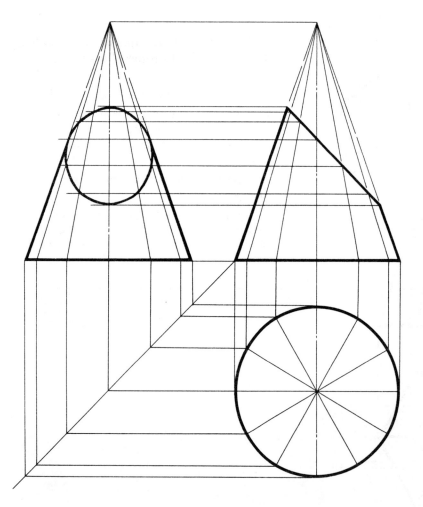

To Draw the End Elevation of the Frustum of a Cone

1. Divide the plan into 12 equal parts. Project each of these points to the base of the cone. Radiate lines from the apex to each of the points on the base.

2. Project horizontal lines from each or the points on the front elevation as shown.

3. Transfer the plan widths to the base of the end elevation, and radiate lines from the apex to these points.

4. Line in the end elevation.

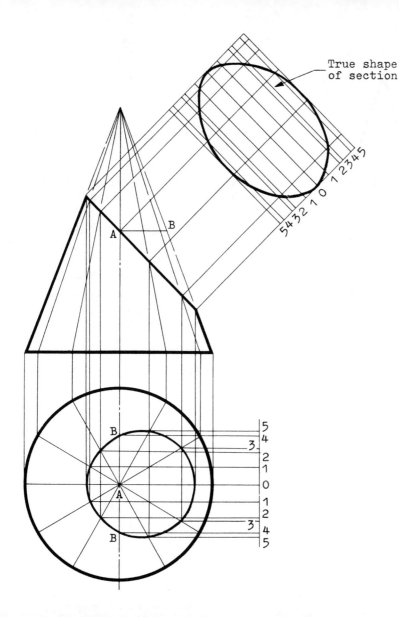

True shape
of section

To Draw the Plan and the True Shape of the Section of a Frustum of a Cone

1. Divide the plan into 12 equal parts. Project these points to the base of the front elevation. Join each of the points on the base to the apex (radiating lines).

2. Project each of the points where the radiating lines cut the section to their corresponding lines on the plan (the widths on the centre lines are found by taking the radius AB from the front elevation). Line in the plan of the section.

3. The true shape of the section is obtained by projecting lines at right angles to the section from each of the points on it, and taking the widths from the plan of the section and then drawing these lines at right angles to those projected from the points on the section.

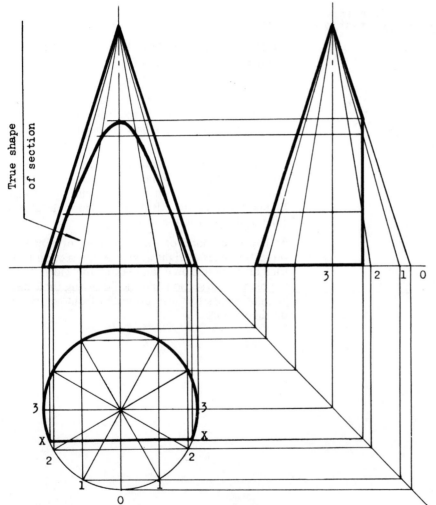

True shape
of section

3 2 1 0

3 3
X X
2 2
1 1
0

To Draw the True Shape of the Vertical Section of a Cone

1. Draw the elevations and the plan of the cone showing the cutting plane of the section on the end elevation and plan.

2. Divide the circumference of the plan into 12 equal parts and project these points to the base of the cone of the front and the end elevations. Radiate lines from the apex to these points.

3. The radiating lines on the end elevation cut the section. Project these points horizontally to cut the corresponding radiating lines on the front elevation. A curve drawn through these points (plus points X X projected from the plan to the base of the front elevation) gives the true shape of the section.

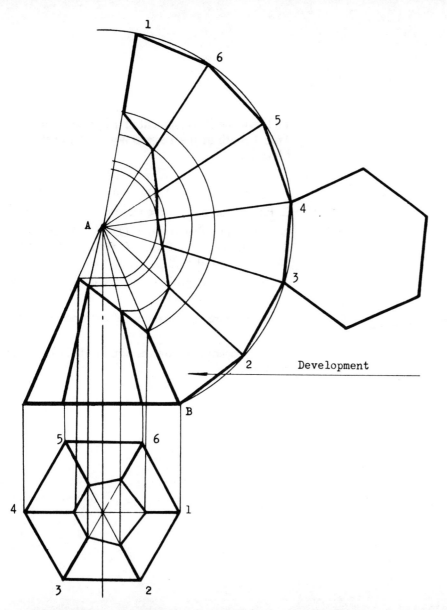

Development

DEVELOPMENTS

To Draw the Development of the Frustum of a Pyramid

1. Draw the elevation and plan.

2. Draw horizontal lines from the edges on the section to touch side AB. With centre A and each point on AB as radius draw arcs.

3. Step the base edges along the arc from B. Draw chords, and connect the points to A.

4. The intersection of the arcs and radiating lines from A mark the top shape.

5. Add the true shape of the section (not shown for clarity) and the base.

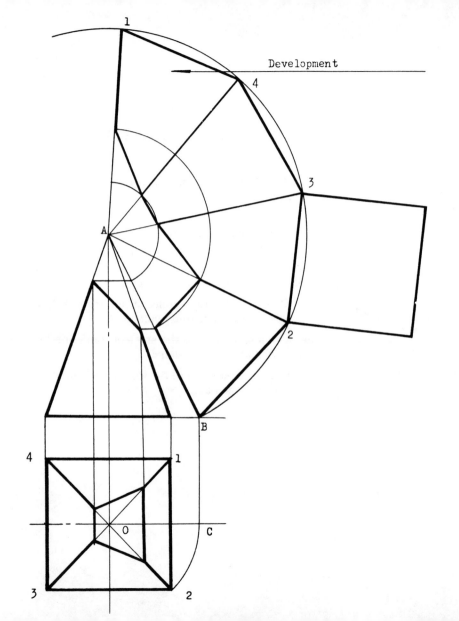

Development

To Draw the Development of a Pyramid when the True Length of the Edge is not shown in the Elevation

1. Draw the elevation and plan of the pyramid.

2. Extend the base of the elevation to the right.

3. With centre O and radius O2 draw an arc to cut the centre line at C. Project C vertically to cut the base extended at B.

4. Join AB and project horizontal line from the edges on the section to it.

5. With centre A and radius of each point on AB draw arcs.

6. The procedure is now the same as in the previous example.

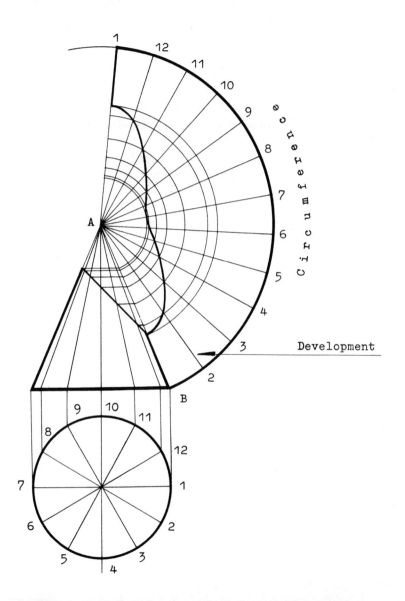

Circumference

Development

To Draw the Development of a Frustum of a Cone

1. Draw the elevation and plan.

2. Divide the plan into 12 equal parts and project these points to the base of the elevation.

3. Radiate lines from A to the points on the base of the elevation. Where the radiating lines cut the section project them horizontally to touch AB.

4. With centre A and each of the points on AB as radius draw arcs.

5. Mark off the plan units 1–12 from B and connect them to A. The intersection of the radiating lines and arcs marks the top shape.

6. Add the base and section (not shown).

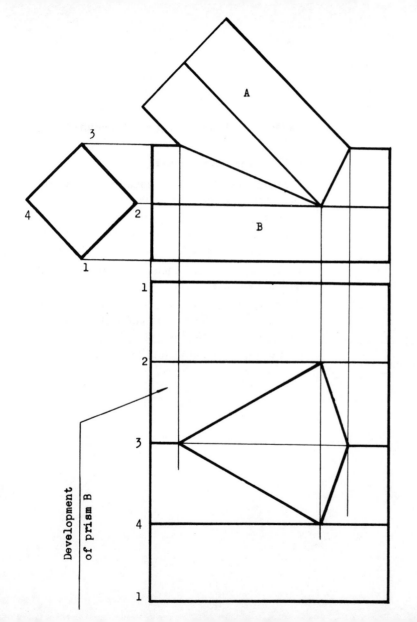

Two Square Prisms are Joined Together as Illustrated. Draw the Development of Prism B

1. Project vertical lines from the elevation. At any convenient distance draw a line parallel to the elevation and mark off the sides 1–2, 2–3, 3–4 and 4–1 from it.

2. Mark the opening in the development.

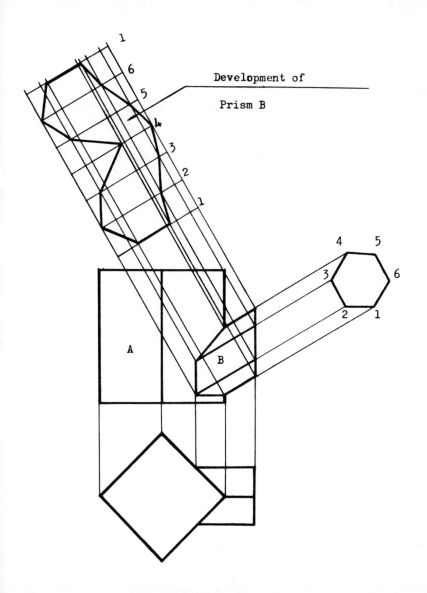

Development of

Prism B

A Hexagonal Prism Joins a Square Prism as Illustrated. Draw the Development of Prism B

1. Project lines perpendicular to the edges of prism B from the points on the elevation.

2. At any convenient distance draw a line parallel to the edges of the prism and mark the sides 1–2, 2–3, 3–4, 4–5, 5–6 and 6–1. The intersection of these lines and the perpendiculars marks the shape of the development.

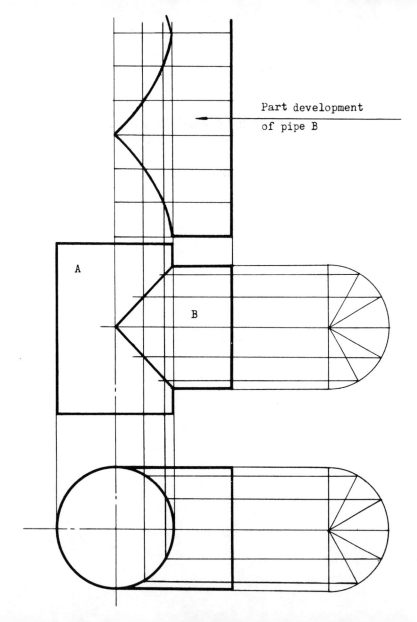

Part development
of pipe B

CURVES OF INTERSECTION

To Draw the Line of Intersection of the Two Cylindrical Pipes of the Same Diameter Joined at Right Angles, and the Development of Pipe B

1. Draw a semicircle at any convenient distance away from the plan and elevation and divide them into 6 equal parts.

2. Project horizontal lines from the points on the plan semicircle to touch the plan of pipe A, and then project these vertically to the elevation. Project horizontal lines from the points on the elevation semicircle to intersect the corresponding vertical projection lines, to mark the line of intersection.

The lines of intersection for two cylinders of the same diameter are always straight lines.

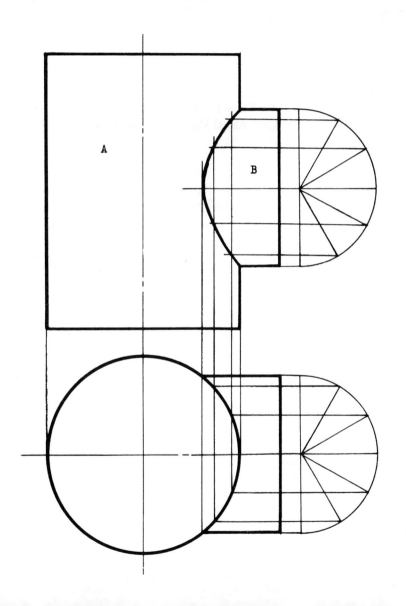

To Draw the Line of Intersection of the Two Cylindrical Pipes of Unequal Diameter Joined at Right Angles

1. Draw a semicircle at any convenient distance away from the plan and elevation and divide them into 6 equal parts.

2. Project horizontal lines from the points on the plan semicircle to touch the plan of pipe A, and then project these vertically to the elevation. Project horizontal lines from the points on the elevation semicircle to intersect the corresponding vertical projection lines, to mark the line of intersection.

The line of intersection of two cylinders of unequal diameter is always a curve.

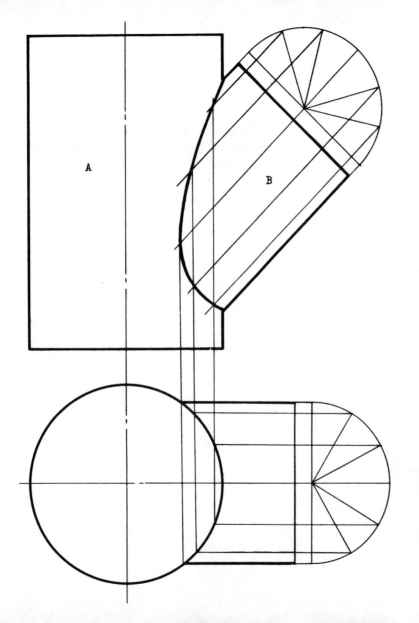

To Draw the Line of Intersection of the Two Cylindrical Pipes of Unequal Diameter Joined at an Angle

1. Draw a semicircle at any convenient distance away from the plan and elevation and divide them into 6 equal parts.

2. Project horizontal lines from the points on the plan semicircle to touch the plan of pipe A, and project these vertically to the elevation. Project lines parallel to pipe B from the points on the elevation semicircle to intersect the corresponding vertical projection lines, to mark the line of intersection.

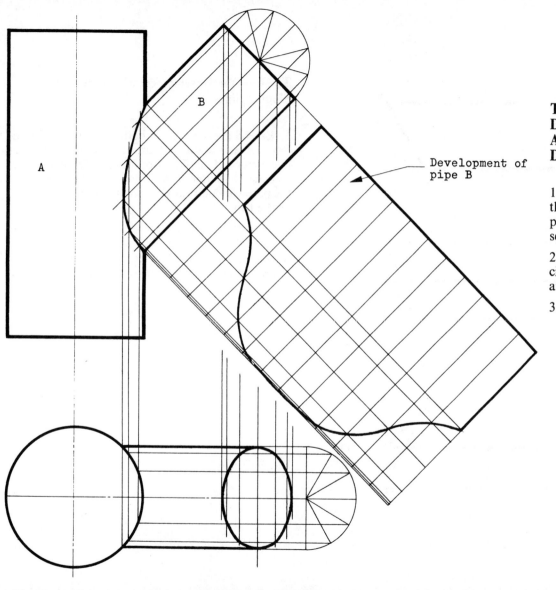

Development of pipe B

B

A

Two Pipes of Unequal Diameter Intersect at an Angle. To Draw the Development of Pipe B

1. Project lines at right angles to the sides of pipe B from each point on the curve of intersection.

2. Draw the 12 divisions (the circumference of pipe B) at right angles to the previous lines.

3. Line in the development.

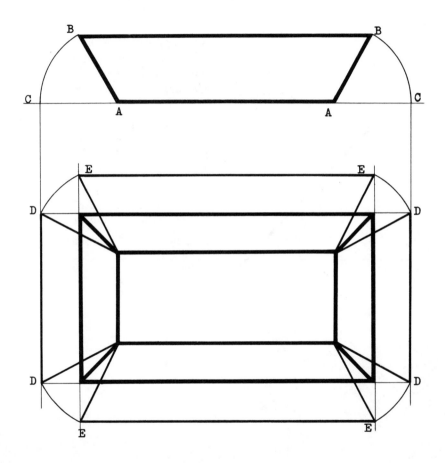

To Draw the Development of a Tray with Sloping Sides

1. Extend the base AA in both directions. With the centre A and radius AB draw an arc to cut the base line extended at C. Drop perpendiculars to the extended base line from C. Produce the sides to cut the perpendiculars at D. Join D to the inside corner of the tray.

2. With the inside corner of the tray as a centre, and a radius of the inside corner—D, draw an arc to cut the end of the tray produced at E. Join E to the inside corner of the tray.

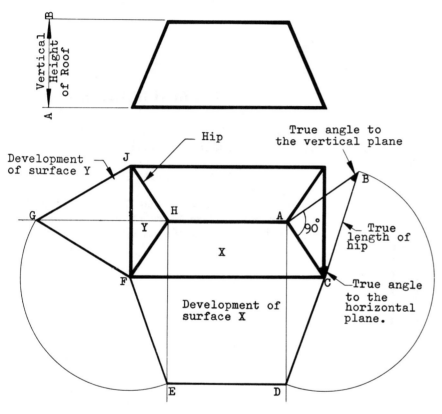

To Find the True Length of the Hip of a Roof and its True Inclination to the Horizontal and Vertical Planes, and also the Development of the Roof Surfaces

1. Take the vertical height, AB, of the roof and draw it perpendicular to the plan of a hip as shown. Join B to C. BC is the true length of the hip.

2. Draw perpendiculars to CF from A and H. With centre C and radius CB draw an arc to cut the perpendicular from A at D. Draw DE parallel to FC, to complete the development of surface X.

3. With centre F and radius FE draw an arc to cut a perpendicular to FJ from H at G. FJG is the development of surface Y.

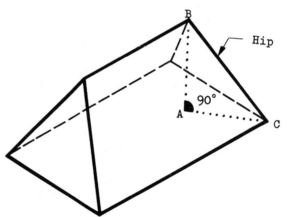

Pictorial view of the roof, illustrating the application of a right-angled triangle to determine the true length of the hip.

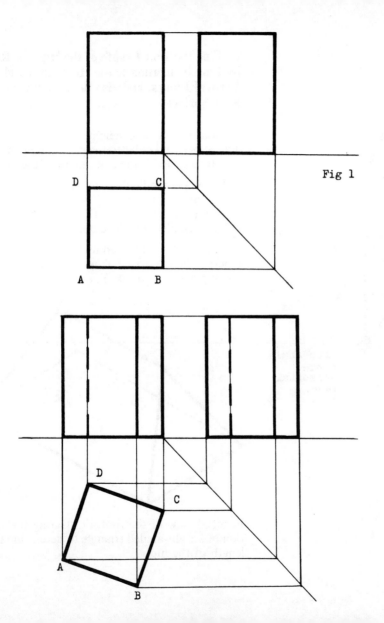

Fig 1

INCLINED SOLIDS

A solid turned at an angle to any of the principal planes is said to be inclined.

Fig. 1 shows a solid parallel to the principal planes.

Turn the solid so that DC is inclined at 15° to the vertical plane. Draw a front and end elevation and a plan. Draw the key view, the plan first.

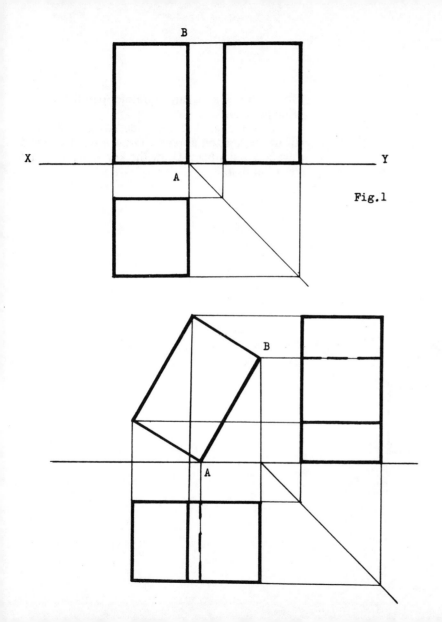

Fig.1

Fig. 1 shows a solid parallel to the principal planes.

Turn the solid so that side AB is inclined at 60° to the horizontal plane. Draw a front and end elevation and a plan. Draw the key view, the front elevation first.

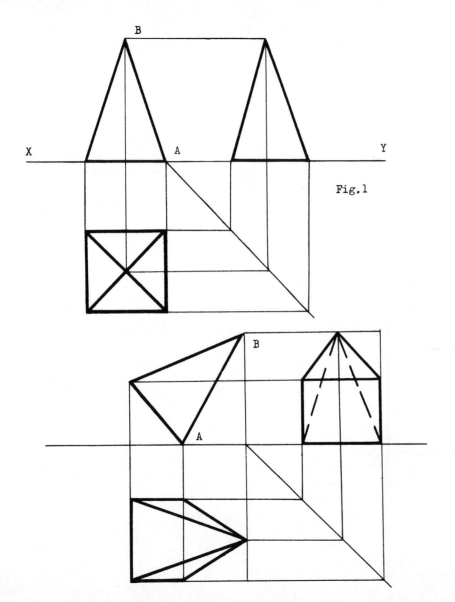

Fig.1

Fig. 1 shows a square pyramid parallel to the principal planes.

Turn the solid so that side AB is inclined at 60° to the horizontal plane. Draw a front and end elevation and a plan. Draw the key view, the front elevation first.

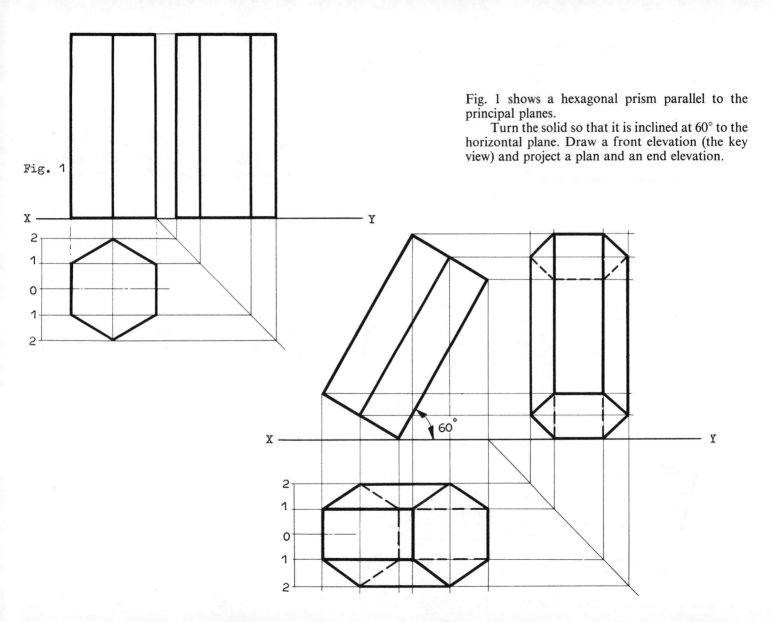

Fig. 1

Fig. 1 shows a hexagonal prism parallel to the principal planes.

Turn the solid so that it is inclined at 60° to the horizontal plane. Draw a front elevation (the key view) and project a plan and an end elevation.

60°

113

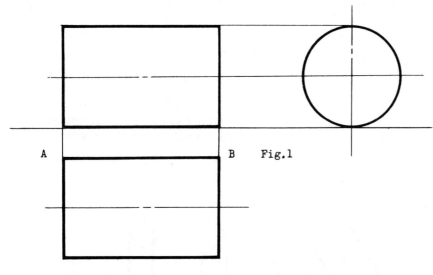

A   B   Fig.1

Fig. 1 shows a cylinder parallel to the principal planes.

Turn the cylinder so that AB is inclined at 20° to the vertical plane. Draw the front and end elevation and a plan.

1. Draw the key view, the plan. Construct a semicircle on AC.

2. Divide AC into an even number of equal parts and project lines parallel to AB to BD.

3. Project the points on AC and BD to the front and end elevations.

4. Take the distances from AC to the semicircle from 1, 2, 3 and mark them each side of a centre line 0 at the front elevation and project horizontal lines to intersect the verticals, thus obtaining the curve points.

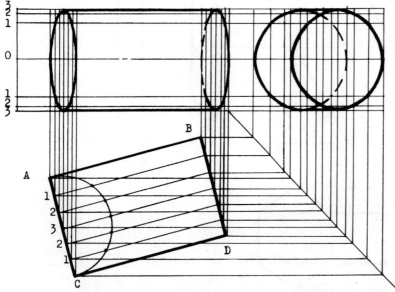

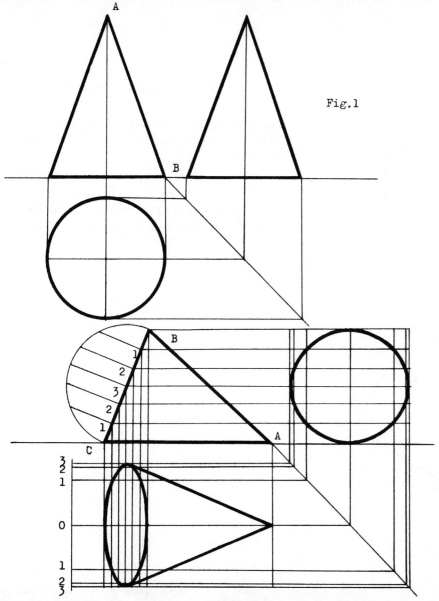

Fig.1

Fig. 1 shows a right cone parallel to the principal planes.

Turn the cone so that AB is resting on the horizontal plane. Draw a front elevation, an end elevation and a plan.

1. Draw the key view, the front elevation, and construct a semicircle on BC.

2. Divide BC into an even number of equal parts and project lines horizontally to the end elevation, vertically to the plan and perpendicular to BC to the semicircle.

3. Take the distances from BC to the semicircle from 1, 2, 3 and mark them each side of a centre line 0 at the plan, and also project them to the end elevation to intersect the lines from BC, thus obtaining the curve points.

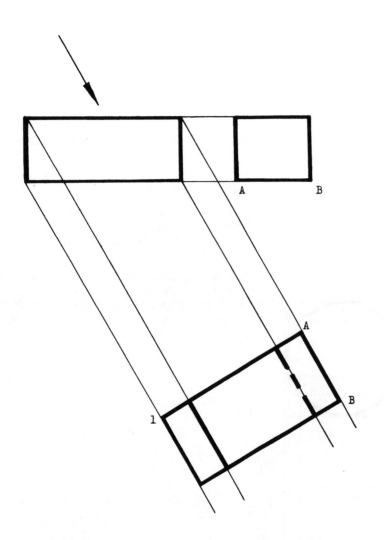

AUXILIARY VIEWS

The front and end elevations of a prism are shown. Draw an auxiliary plan looking in the direction of the arrow.

1. Project lines from the points on the front elevation parallel to the arrow.

2. At any convenient distance draw a line 1A perpendicular to the arrow and mark the plan width AB. Line in the auxiliary view.

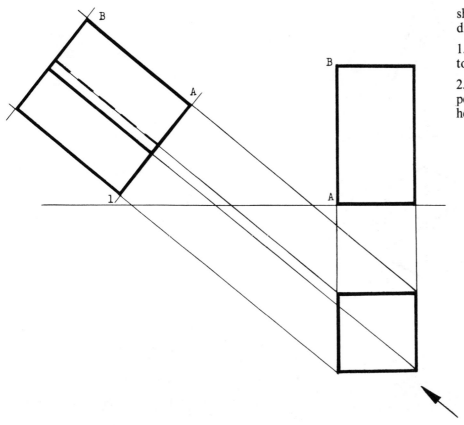

The front elevation and the plan of a prism are shown. Draw an auxiliary elevation looking in the direction of the arrow.

1. Project lines from the points on the plan parallel to the arrow.

2. At any convenient distance draw a line 1A perpendicular to the arrow and mark the elevation height AB. Line in the auxiliary view.

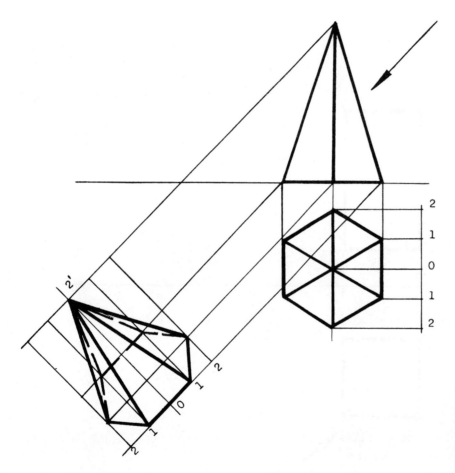

The front elevation and the plan of a hexagonal pyramid are shown. Draw an auxiliary plan looking in the direction of the arrow.

1. Mark the plan widths 01, 02.

2. Draw lines from the points on the front elevation parallel to the arrow.

3. At any convenient distance draw line 02′ perpendicular to the arrow and mark the plan widths 01, 02 each side of it. Line in the auxiliary view.

118

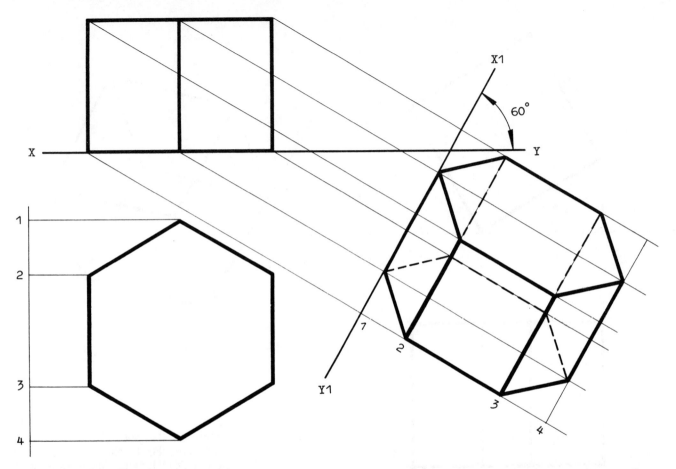

The front elevation and the plan of a hexagonal prism are shown. Draw an auxiliary plan on the ground line X1Y1.

1. Mark the plan widths 1, 2, 3, 4.

2. Draw the ground line X1Y1, and project lines at right angles to it from each point on front elevation.

3. Transfer the plan widths 1, 2, 3, 4 to the auxiliary plan as shown.

4. Line in the auxiliary plan.

119

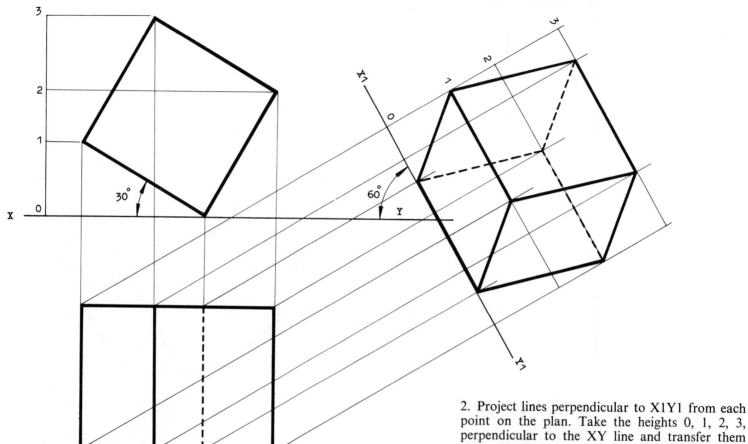

Given the front elevation of a cube inclined to the horizontal plane, draw an auxiliary elevation on the ground line X1Y1.

1. Draw the given front elevation, and project a plan. Draw X1Y1.

2. Project lines perpendicular to X1Y1 from each point on the plan. Take the heights 0, 1, 2, 3, perpendicular to the XY line and transfer them above X1Y1. The intersection of the lines from the plan with their corresponding height lines gives the points for the required auxiliary elevation.

If we are asked to draw an auxiliary plan, we project lines from the front elevation; and if we are asked to draw an auxiliary elevation, we project lines from the plan.

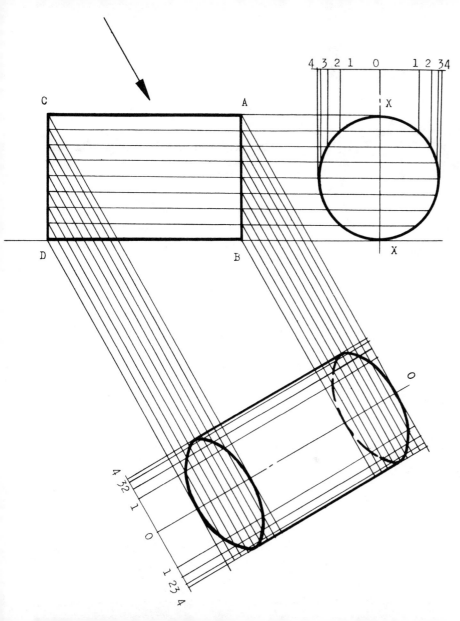

The front and end elevations of a cylinder are shown. Draw an auxiliary plan looking in the direction of the arrow.

1. Divide the vertical diameter XX of the end elevation into an even number of equal parts and project horizontal lines to the front elevation ends AB and CD.

2. Project lines from the points on AB and CD parallel to the arrow.

3. At any convenient distance draw line 00 perpendicular to the arrow.

4. Mark the end elevation widths 01, 02, 03, 04 and transfer them each side of line 00 on the plan.

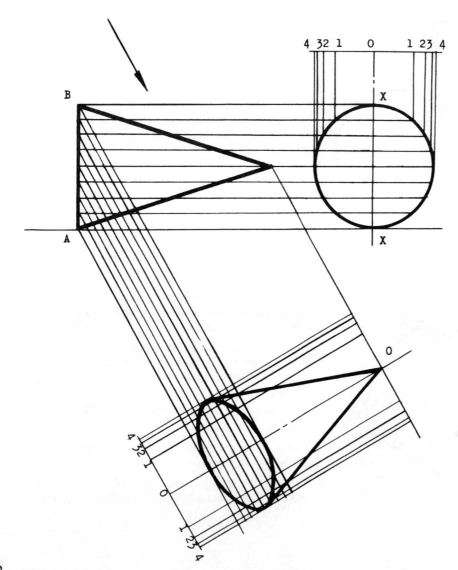

The front and end elevations of a cone are shown. Draw an auxiliary plan looking in the direction of the arrow.

1. Divide the vertical diameter XX of the end elevation into an even number of equal parts and project horizontal lines to touch base AB.

2. Project lines from the points on AB parallel to the arrow.

3. At any convenient distance draw centre line 00 perpendicular to the arrow.

4. Mark the end elevation widths 01, 02, 03, 04 and transfer them each side of centre line 00 on the plan.

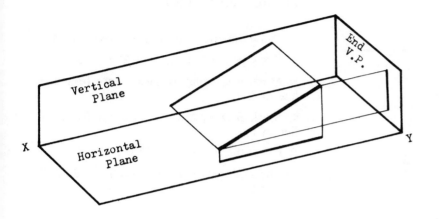

LINES IN SPACE

It is often necessary to find the true length of a line and its angles to the planes.

If a line makes an angle to a plane it will, if produced, penetrate the plane. The point where it penetrates the plane is called the trace.

To Find the Traces of a Line Given the Elevation and Plan of the Line

1. Produce the elevation to the XY line and project this point to the plan produced. This point is the horizontal trace (H.T.).

2. Produce the plan to the XY line and project this point to the elevation produced. This point is called the vertical trace (V.T.).

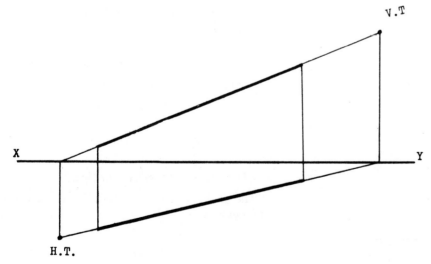

123

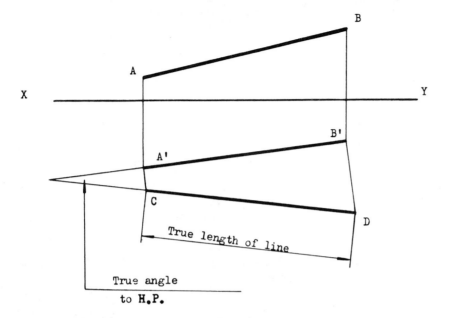

To Find the True Length of a Line and its True Angle to the Horizontal Plane, Given the Elevation and the Plan

1. Draw the given elevation AB and plan A'B'.

2. Draw perpendiculars to A'B' at A' and B'.

3. Mark A'C equal to the distance from the XY line to A.

4. Mark B'D equal to the distance from the XY line to B.

5. CD is the true length of the line.

6. The angle between A'B' and CD produced is the true angle to the H.P.

To Find the True Length of a Line and its True Angle to the Vertical Plane Given the Elevation and the Plan

1. Draw the given elevation AB and plan A'B'.

2. Draw perpendiculars to AB at A and B.

3. Mark AC equal to the distance from the XY line to A'.

4. Mark BD equal to the distance from the XY line to B'.

5. CD is the true length of the line.

6. The angle between AB and CD extended is the true angle to the V.P.

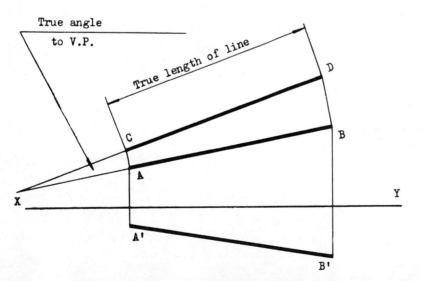

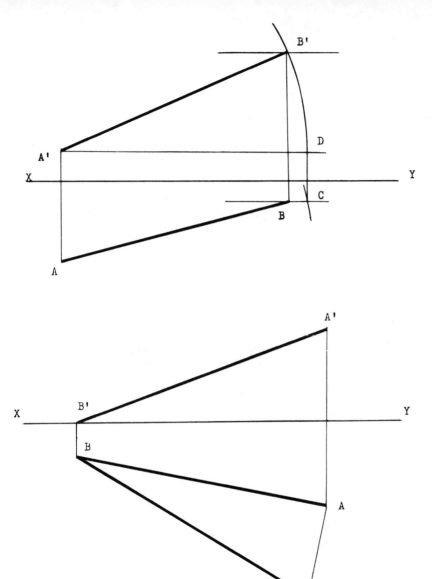

To Draw the Elevation and Plan of a Line, Given its True Length and the Distance of its ends from the Planes

1. Let the true length of the line be 83 mm. One end of the line 6 mm in front of the V.P. and 41 mm above the H.P., the other end of the line 25 mm in front of the V.P. and 10 mm above the H.P.

2. Draw a perpendicular projector to XY and mark A 25 mm below the XY and A' 10 mm above it.

3. Draw a line parallel to XY, 6 mm below it. With centre A and radius 83 mm draw an arc to cut the parallel line at C.

4. Draw a line parallel to XY from A'.

5. Draw a line 41 mm above XY and parallel to it.

6. Draw a vertical projector from C to touch the parallel from A' at D.

7. With centre A' and radius A'D draw an arc to cut the parallel line at B'. A'B' is the elevation of the line.

8. Drop a vertical projector from B', to cut the parallel at B. AB is the plan of the line.

To Draw the Elevation of a Line, Given the Plan and the True Inclination to the H.P.

1. Draw the given plan AB.

2. Erect a perpendicular to AB at A.

3. Construct the angle ABC equal to the given angle to the H.P.

4. Draw perpendicular projectors to XY from A and B.

5. Mark XY to A' equal to AC.

6. A'B' is the required elevation.

125

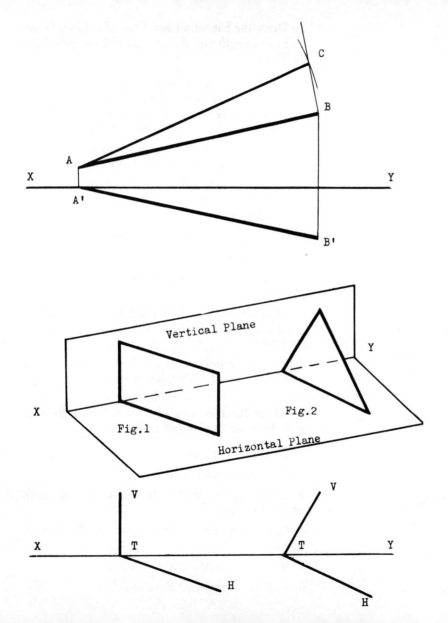

To Draw the Plan of a Line Given the Elevation and the True Length

1. Draw the given elevation AB.

2. Draw a perpendicular to AB at B.

3. With centre A and radius equal to the given length of line draw an arc to cut the perpendicular at C.

4. Mark XY to B′ equal to BC.

5. A′B′ is the required plan.

TRACES OF PLANES

An inclined plane (Fig. 1) is inclined to one of the principal planes and perpendicular to the other.

An oblique plane (Fig. 2) is inclined to both of the principal planes.

The lines traced on the horizontal and vertical planes by the plane are known as the traces.

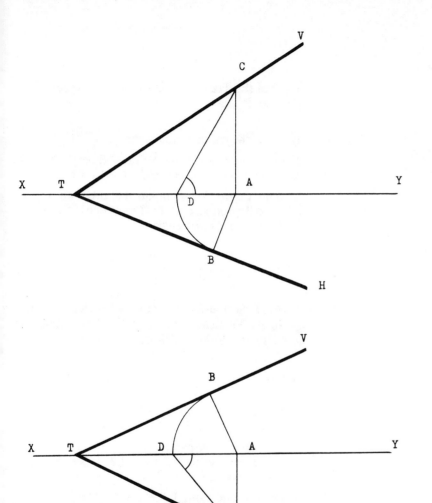

To Find the Angle Between the Oblique Plane and the Horizontal Plane

1. Draw the vertical trace (V.T.) and the horizontal trace (H.T.) of the plane.

2. From any point A on XY draw AB perpendicular to the H.T.

3. From A draw a perpendicular to XY to touch the V.T. at C.

4. With centre A and radius AB draw an arc to touch XY at D. Join CD. Angle CDA is the required angle.

To Find the Angle Between an Oblique Plane and the Vertical Plane

1. Draw the vertical and horizontal traces.

2. From any point A on XY draw AB perpendicular to the V.T.

3. From A draw a perpendicular to XY to touch the H.T. at C.

4. With centre A and radius AB draw an arc to touch XY at D. Join CD. Angle CDA is the required angle.

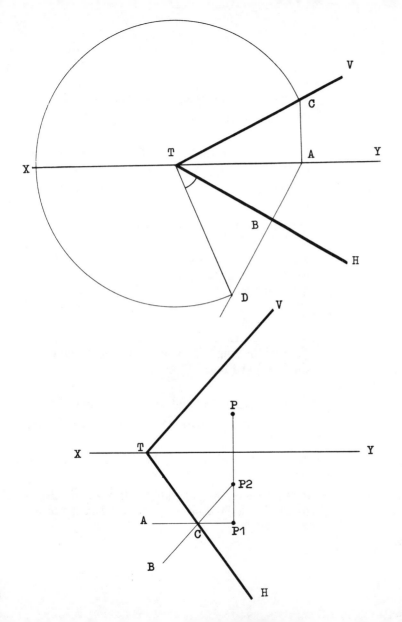

To Find the True Angle Between the Traces of an Oblique Plane

1. Draw the traces of the plane.

2. From any point A on XY draw AB perpendicular to the H.T. and AC perpendicular to XY.

3. With centre T and radius TC draw an arc to touch AB produced at D. Draw line TD. Angle DTH is the required angle.

To Find the Horizontal Trace of a Plane when given its Vertical Trace and the Projections (P and P1) of a Point which Lies in the Plane

1. Draw the given V.T. and the projections P and P1 of the Point in the plane.

2. Mark P2, by making P1P2 equal to the perpendicular distance of P from the XY line.

3. Draw line P1A parallel to XY from P1. Draw line P2B parallel to VT from P2. Lines P2B and P1A intersect at C.

4. Draw a line from T through C. This line is the required H.T.

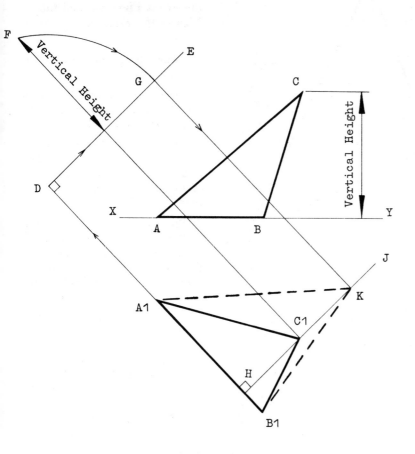

To Find the True Shape of a Triangle when Given the Plan and the Elevation and that One Edge Lies on the Horizontal Plane

1. Draw the given front elevation and plan of the triangle (edge AB rests on the H.P.).

2. Extend A1 B1 to any convenient length (B1D). Draw a perpendicular to B1D at D (DE).

3. Extend a line parallel to B1D from C1 and mark the 'vertical height' on it from DE to give point F.

4. With centre D and radius DF draw an arc to touch DE at G.

5. Draw a line perpendicular to B1D through C1 (HJ).

6. Draw a line parallel to B1D from G to touch HJ at K. A1B1K is the required true shape of the triangle.

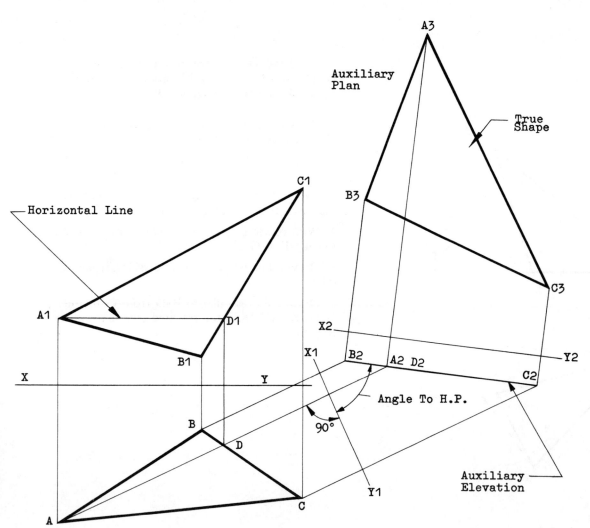

Auxiliary
Plan

True
Shape

A3

B3

C3

Horizontal Line

C1

A1

D1

B1

X2

Y2

X1

B2   A2 D2

C2

X   Y

Angle To H.P.

90°

B

D

Auxiliary
Elevation

A

C

Y1

To Find the True Shape of any Triangle and its Angle to the Horizontal Plane When Given the Front Elevation and the Plan of the Triangle

1. Draw the given front elevation and plan.

2. Draw a horizontal line from A1 (A1D1) and project the plan of this line, AD.

3. Extend line AD and draw lines parallel to it from B and C. Draw X1Y1 perpendicular to AD extended at any convenient place.

4. Project an auxiliary elevation A2B2C2 from the plan (project at right angles to X1Y1), making the distance of A2 from the X1Y1=the perpendicular distance of A1 from XY, etc.

5. Draw a ground line X2Y2 Parallel to line A2B2C2 at any convenient place and project an auxiliary plan, making the distance of A3 from X2Y2=the distance of A from X1Y1, etc. The triangle A3B3C3 is the required true shape.

The true shape of the triangle can also be found by finding the true length of each side in turn.

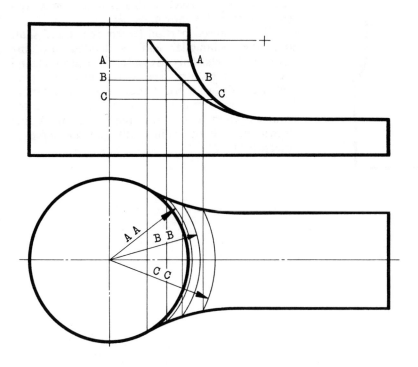

The curve of intersection that is found on cranks and levers is shown.

A series of sections are indicated on the front elevation and the radius of each of these is set out on the plan and arcs are drawn to touch the sides of the crank. These points are projected back to the front elevation to cut their relevant lines. A line drawn through the points will give the curve of intersection.

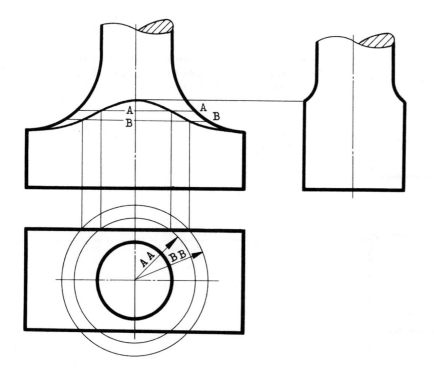

The curve of intersection that is found on a connecting-rod end is shown.

The radiused portion (where the round shaft joins the rectangular end) is divided into any number of parts. This gives a series of sections, and the radius of each of these is set out on the plan and circles drawn to touch the sides of the rectangular end. These points are projected back to the front elevation to cut their relevant lines. A line drawn through the points will give the curve of intersection.

ARCHES

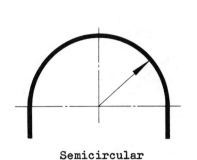

Semicircular

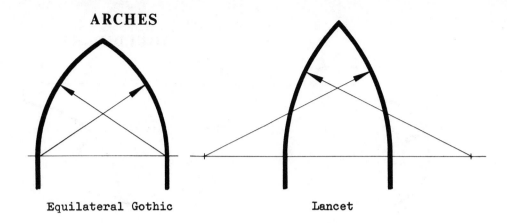

Equilateral Gothic

Lancet

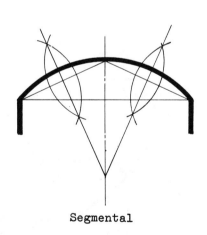

Segmental

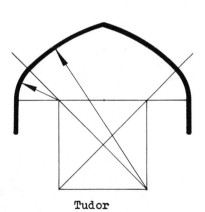

Tudor

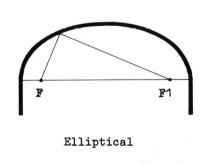

Elliptical

This is a method of drawing a tudor arch when given the span. Divide the span into 4 equal parts and below the centre 2 parts construct a square. The diagonals of the square are common normals to the curve.

MOULDINGS

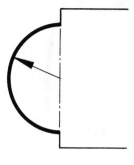

Astral or Bead

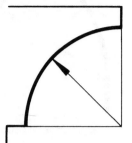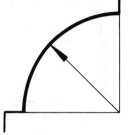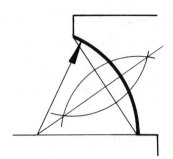

Cavetto

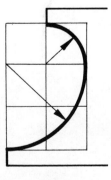

Scotia

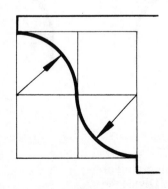

Cyma Recta

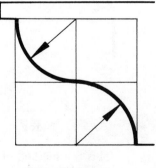

Cyma Reversa

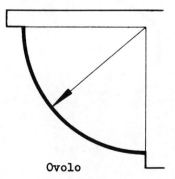

Ovolo

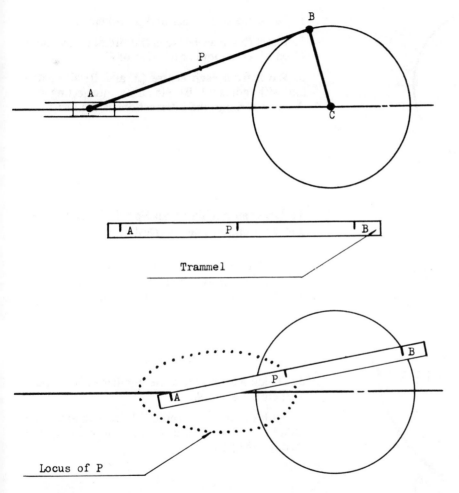

Trammel

Locus of P

LOCI

A locus is a clearly defined path and is either a straight line or curve. Loci is the plural of locus.

A locus is a path traced by a point moving in accordance with a definite rule.

The locus of a piece of machinery composed of links can be traced with a paper trammel. In other cases the locus can be drawn with the use of a pair of compasses.

A crank BC rotates about a fixed centre C. A rod AB is pin-jointed to the crank at B and freely slides in guides at end A. Draw the locus of a point P on AB for one revolution of the crank.

1. Mark AB and the point P on it on a piece of paper, the trammel.

2. Draw a circle of radius BC with a horizontal diameter extended.

3. Use the trammel so that A remains on the centre line while B moves round the circle. Point P will trace the locus.

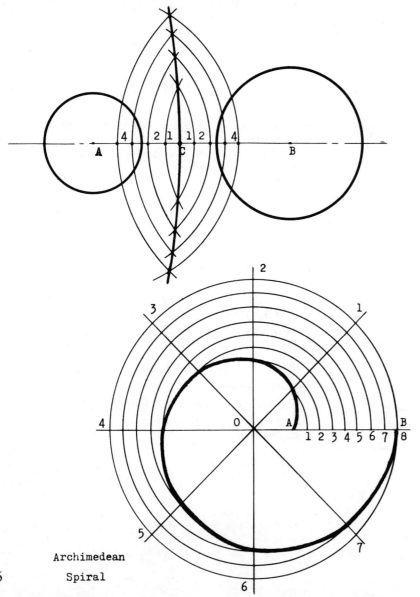

To Draw the Locus of a Point so that its Distance from Two Circles is Equal

1. Draw the two circles and join their centres.

2. Bisect the space between the circles to give point C. Mark equal units each side of C.

3. Work from each centre (A and B) alternately and with radius A1, B1, etc., draw intersecting arcs. A curve through the intersections is the locus.

To Draw an Archimedean Spiral, Given the Pole and the Longest and Shortest Radii

1. An Archimedean spiral is the path of a point moving uniformly along a straight line rotating about a fixed point at an even speed.

   Mark the pole 0. Draw 0A and 0B equal to the given radii.

2. With centre 0 and radius 0B draw a circle and divide it into 8 equal sectors.

3. Divide AB into the same number of equal parts as there are sectors.

4. With centre 0 and radius 01 draw an arc to cut radial 1. Repeat for 2, 3, 4, 5, 6, 7, 8. Draw a curve through the points.

Archimedean Spiral

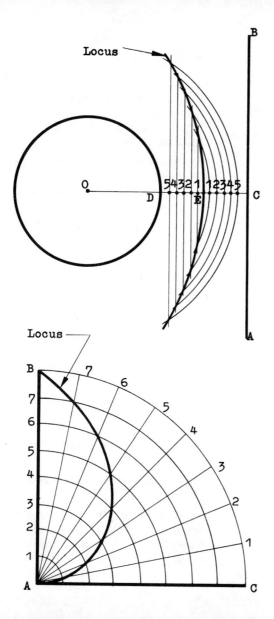

To Draw the Locus of a Point so that its Distance from a Circle and a Straight Line is Always Equal

1. Draw the given circle with centre O and the straight line AB.

2. Draw a line from O perpendicular to AB (line OC). D is the point where the circumference of the circle cuts line OC. Bisect DC to give point E. Mark units of equal length (1, 2, 3, 4, 5) each side of E. Draw lines from the points to the left of E parallel to line AB, and with centre O and radii O1, O2, O3, O4, O5 (points 1, 2, 3, 4, 5, to the right of E), draw arcs to intersect their corresponding straight lines. Draw the locus through the intersections.

The locus is the centre of circles to touch the given circle and straight line AB.

A rod AB pivots about A and moves through 90° to AC at uniform speed. At the same time a point (P) starts at B and slides along the rod at uniform speed to reach A at the same time that the road reaches its final position. Draw the locus of the point (P).

1. Draw the rod AB, and also the rod in its final position, AC.

2. With centre A and radius AB draw the arc BC.

3. Divide AB and the arc CB into the same number of equal parts. Radiate lines from the points on the arc to A. With centre A, and radii A1, A2, A3, A4, A5, on AB, draw arcs to AC. The intersections of the arcs with their corresponding radial lines give the points for the locus.

137

Cycloid

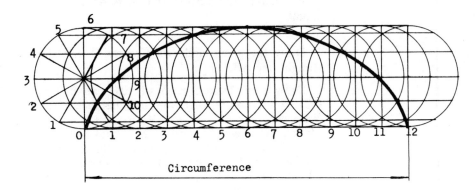

Circumference

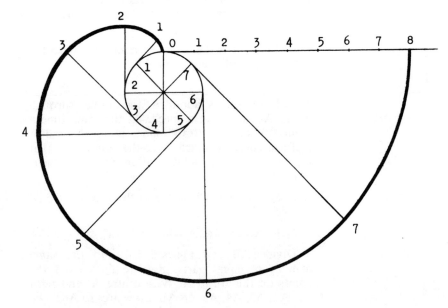

Involute of Circle

To Draw a Cycloid

1. A cycloid is the path of a point on the circumference of a circle rolling along a straight line. Draw the circle and divide the circumference into 12 equal parts.

2. Draw horizontal lines from 0, 1, 2, 3, . . . Divide the line from 0 into the same 12 units as the circumference of the circle and erect perpendiculars.

3. With the intersection of the perpendiculars 1, 2, 3, 4, . . . and the horizontal circle centre line as centres, draw circles the same radius as the first circle.

4. Circle with centre perpendicular 1 cuts horizontal line 1 and circle with centre perpendicular 2 cuts horizontal line 2, etc. A curve drawn through these points gives the required cycloid.

To Draw the Involute of a Circle

1. The involute of a circle is the path traced by the free end of a thread as it is unwound from the circle.
   Draw the circle and divide the circumference into any number of equal parts (8 shown).

2. Draw tangents at 0, 1, 2, . . . At 0 mark off the same number of equal spaces as the circumference of the circle is divided into.

3. Mark the length of the tangent from 1 of 1 unit length, the length of the tangent from 2 of 2 units length, etc. A curve drawn through these points is the required involute.

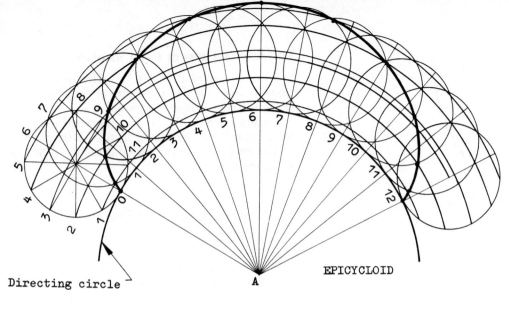

EPICYCLOID

Directing circle

To Draw an Epicycloid

An epicycloid is the locus of a point on the circumference of a circle as it rolls, without slipping, around the outside of a larger circle.

The method of construction is similar to that for the cycloid on page 138.

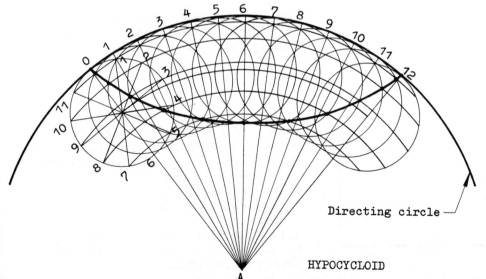

Directing circle

HYPOCYCLOID

To Draw a Hypocycloid

A hypocycloid is the locus of a point on the circumference of a circle as it rolls, without slipping, around the inside of a larger circle.

The method of construction is similar to that for the cycloid on page 138.

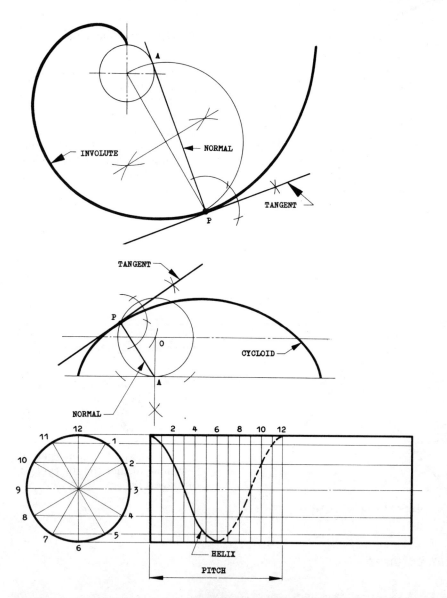

To Draw a Tangent to an Involute

1. From the point P, where you wish to draw the tangent, draw a line to the centre of the base circle; and construct a semi-circle on this line.
2. Draw a line from P to A, the point where the semi-circle circle cuts the base circle. This line is the normal.
3. The tangent is drawn by constructing a line at 90° to the normal.

To Draw a Tangent to a Cycloid

1. From the point P, where you wish to draw the tangent, draw an arc of radius equal to the rolling circle, to cut the centre line at O.
2. With centre O, draw the rolling circle, which touches the base line at A.
3. PA is the normal. The tangent is drawn by constructing a line at 90° to the normal.

The tangent to an epi-cycloid and a hypo-cycloid is obtained in exactly the same way as for a cycloid.

To Draw a Helix

1. A helix is the path of a point moving round a cylinder and at the same time axially, with the ratio of the two movements constant. Draw a circle of diameter equal to the cylinder, and divide the circumference into 12 equal parts.
2. Draw the front elevation of the cylinder and project horizontal lines from 1, 2, 3, . . . on the end elevation.
3. Divide the pitch into 12 equal parts. These lines intersect their corresponding horizontal lines, thus marking the curve points.

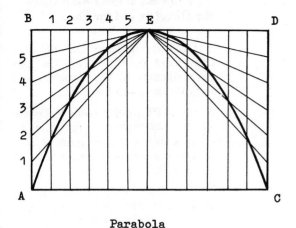

Parabola

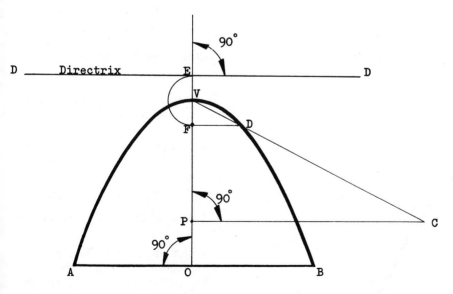

To Draw a Parabola, Given the Span and Height

1. Divide AB, DC, half-span BE and half-span ED into 6 equal parts.

2. With centre E radiate lines to 1, 2, . . .

3. Draw vertical lines from the points on BD to intersect their corresponding radial lines to mark the curve points.

To find the Focus and the Directrix of a Parabola

1. Bisect AB to give point O.

2. Draw a perpendicular to AB at O. V is the vertex. Mark P at any convenient point, and draw PC perpendicular to OV and twice the length PV.

3. Join C to V. This line cuts the curve at D.

4. Draw a perpendicular to OV from D to determine the focus F.

5. With centre V and radius VF draw a semicircle to cut OV extended at E.

6. Draw a perpendicular to OE at E. This line is the directrix DD.

141

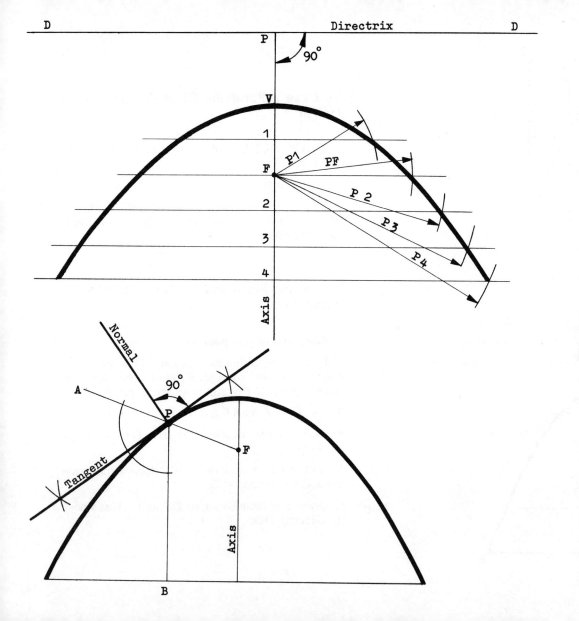

To Draw a Parabola when Given the Directrix and the Focus

1. Draw the directrix DD and at a convenient point P draw the axis perpendicular to the directrix and indicate the given focus F.

2. Bisect PF to give point V. Divide VF into two equal parts and take one of these units and mark points 2, 3, 4, on the axis. Draw perpendiculars to the axis from the points on it.

3. With centre F and P1 as a radius draw an arc each side of the axis to cut line 1. Repeat the procedure as shown. Draw the parabola through the points.

A parabola is the locus of a point which moves so that its distance from the focus equals its perpendicular distance from the directrix.

To Draw a Tangent to a Parabola at a Given Point on the Curve

1. Draw the parabola and indicate the focus F and the given point P on the curve.

2. Draw PB parallel to the axis.

3. Extend a line from F through P (PA).

4. Bisect angle BPA. The bisector is the required tangent. A normal is a line perpendicular to the tangent from P.

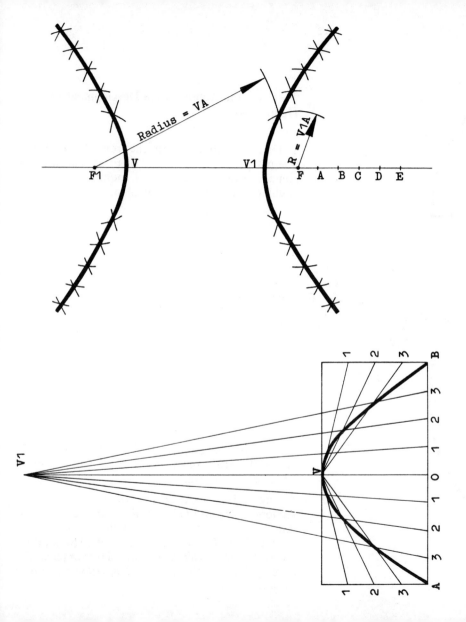

To Draw a Hyperbola when Given the Foci and the Transverse Axis

1. Draw the given foci F and F1, and the transverse axis VV1.

2. Take any convenient unit and mark it off from F to give points A, B, C, D, E.

3. Use radius VA from one focal point and radius V1A from the other focal point to obtain the four points on the hyperbolic curve. The other points are obtained by using radii B, etc.

   A tangent at a given point P on the curve is obtained by joining P to the focal points F and F1 and then bisecting the angle FPF1. The bisector is the required tangent.

To Draw a Hyperbola when Given the Ordinate, the Vertex and the Transverse Axis

1. Indicate O and mark the ordinate each side of it, OA and OB.

2. At O draw a perpendicular to AB and mark the vertex V and the transverse axis VV1.

3. Divide OA, OB, and the two perpendiculars at A and B into the same number of equal parts. Radiate lines as shown. The intersection of the lines gives the points for the hyperbolic curve.

143

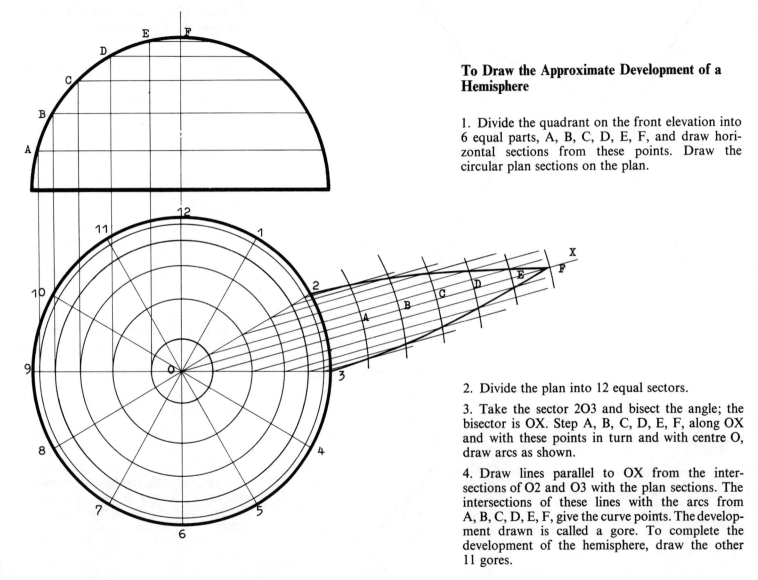

To Draw the Approximate Development of a Hemisphere

1. Divide the quadrant on the front elevation into 6 equal parts, A, B, C, D, E, F, and draw horizontal sections from these points. Draw the circular plan sections on the plan.

2. Divide the plan into 12 equal sectors.

3. Take the sector 2O3 and bisect the angle; the bisector is OX. Step A, B, C, D, E, F, along OX and with these points in turn and with centre O, draw arcs as shown.

4. Draw lines parallel to OX from the intersections of O2 and O3 with the plan sections. The intersections of these lines with the arcs from A, B, C, D, E, F, give the curve points. The development drawn is called a gore. To complete the development of the hemisphere, draw the other 11 gores.

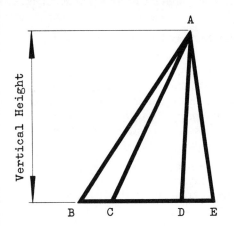

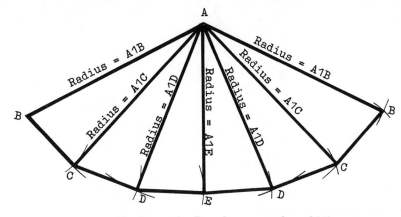

To Draw the Development of an Oblique Pyramid

1. The edges AB and AE are their true lengths on the front elevation. It is necessary to find the true lengths of the remaining edges by the method shown.

2. To draw the development first draw any line equal in length to the true length of AE. With centre A and radius A1D (the true length of AD) describe an arc each side of AE, then with centre E and radius ED (the length of one side of the base) describe an arc to cut each of the previous arcs. Next, with centre A and radius A1C describe an arc to the side of AD, then with centre D and radius DC describe an arc to cut the previous arc. Next, with centre A and radius A1B (the true length of AB) describe an arc to the side of AC, then with centre C and radius CB draw an arc to cut the previous one. Join the points to complete the development.

If the base of the pyramid is required, this may be added by constructing a regular hexagon on any one of the base edges.

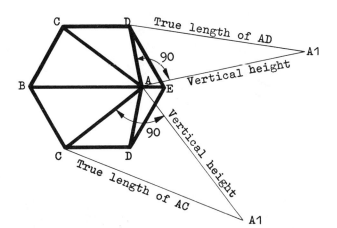

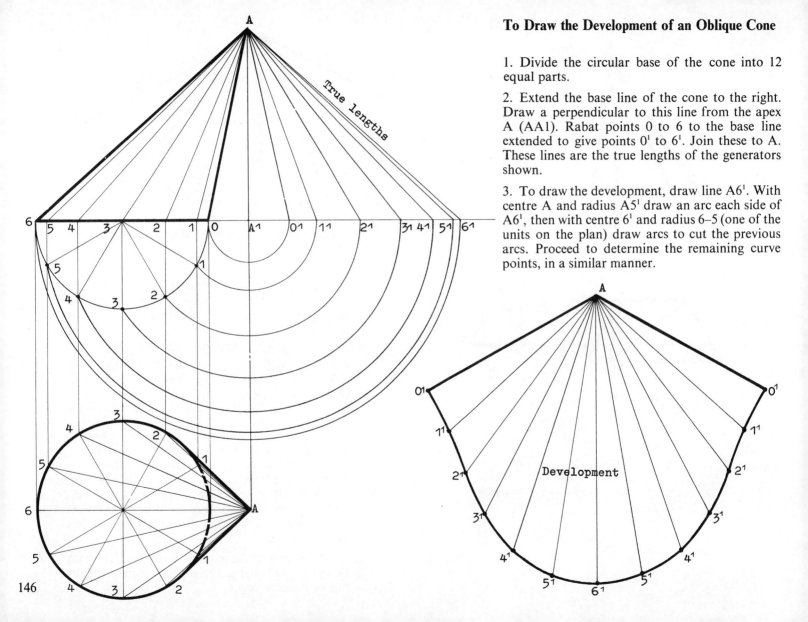

To Draw the Development of an Oblique Cone

1. Divide the circular base of the cone into 12 equal parts.

2. Extend the base line of the cone to the right. Draw a perpendicular to this line from the apex A (AA1). Rabat points 0 to 6 to the base line extended to give points 0^1 to 6^1. Join these to A. These lines are the true lengths of the generators shown.

3. To draw the development, draw line $A6^1$. With centre A and radius $A5^1$ draw an arc each side of $A6^1$, then with centre 6^1 and radius 6–5 (one of the units on the plan) draw arcs to cut the previous arcs. Proceed to determine the remaining curve points, in a similar manner.

True lengths

Development

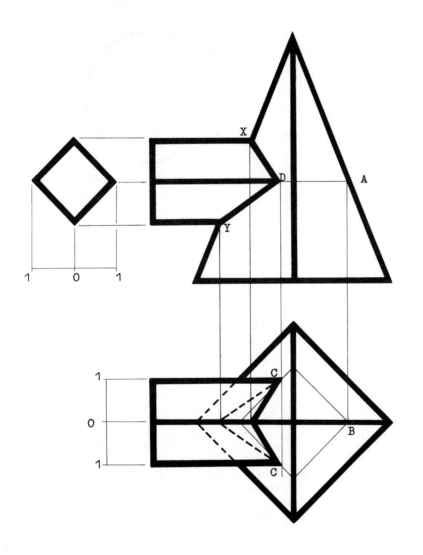

To Draw the Lines of Intersection of a Square Prism Intersecting a Square Pyramid

1. Extend the centre line of the square prism to touch the edge of the pyramid at A. Project a vertical line from A to touch the edge on the plan at B. From this point draw a square parallel to the pyramid plan.

2. Take the widths O–1 from the end elevation of the square prism and place them about the centre line of the plan. The intersection of the lines 1 with the square from B gives the required points C. Project C to the centre line of the square prism on the front elevation, to give point D.

3. Drop perpendiculars from X and Y to the centre line of the plan.

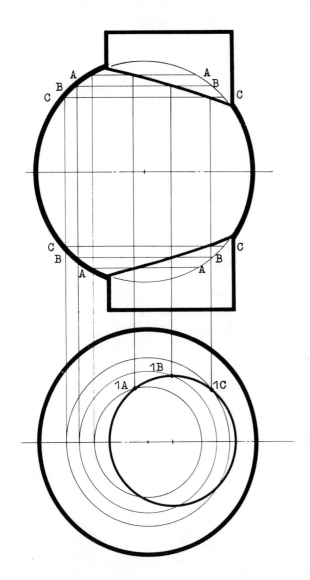

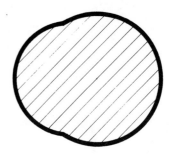

The horizontal sections produce intersecting circles.

To Draw the Curve of Intersection when a Cylinder Pierces a Sphere and when their Vertical Axes do not Coincide

1. Draw any series of sections AA, BB, CC. Draw the plans of these sections.

2. The intersections of the plans of the sections with the plan of the cylinder gives the points 1A, 1B, 1C. These points are then projected to their corresponding horizontal sections on the front elevation, to determine the curve points.

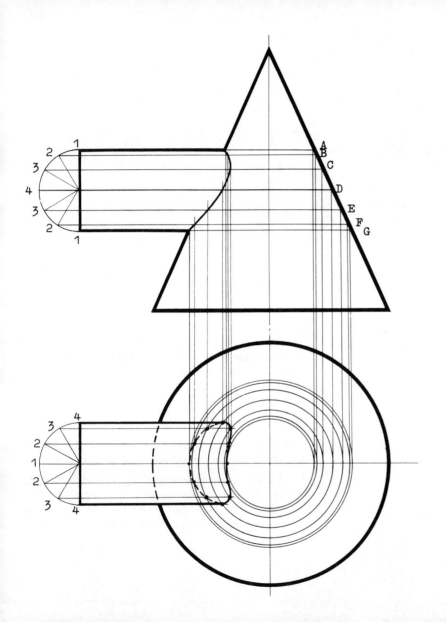

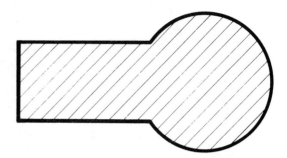

The horizontal sections produce
intersecting circles and rectangles

To Draw the Curves of Intersection of a Cylinder Intersecting a Cone as shown

1. Draw the horizontal sections 1A, 2B, 3C, 4D, 3E, 2F, 1G.

2. Project the points A, B, C, D, E, F, G, to the centre line of the plan and draw the circular cone sections.

3. The intersection of the cone sections with their corresponding cylinder sections gives the points for the curve on the plan. These points are then projected to their corresponding lines on the front elevation, to give the curve points on the front elevation.

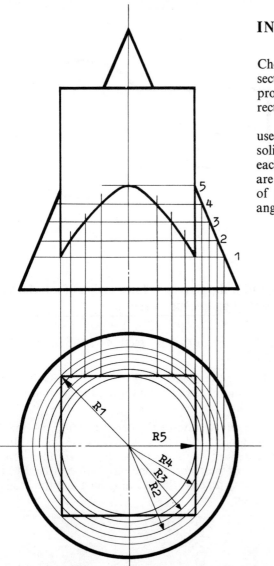

INTERPENETRATIONS

Choose horizontal or vertical sections depending on which produces the easiest shapes, e.g., rectangles and circles, etc.

Vertical sections are usually used when the axes of the two solids are at an oblique angle to each other. Horizontal sections are usually used when the axes of the two solids are at right angles to each other.

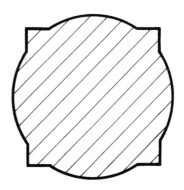

The horizontal sections produce intersecting circles and squares

To Draw the Curve of Interpenetration of a Square Prism Pierced by a Cone

1. Draw the plan sections R1 and R5. Draw the intermediate plan sections R2, R3, R4.

2. Project the plan sections to the side of the cone and draw the horizontal sections, 1, 2, 3, 4, 5.

3. The plan sections intersect the plan of the square prism. Project these points to intersect their corresponding horizontal sections on the front elevation. These are the curve points.

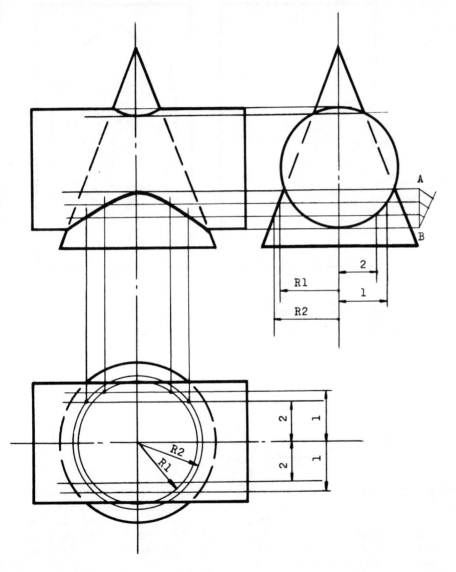

To Draw the Curve of Intersection of a Horizontal Cylinder Intersected by a Right Cone

1. Draw a plan and elevation of the cylinder and cone.

2. Divide the vertical height AB of the extremities of the curve of intersection shown on the end elevation into a number of equal units, and project these horizontally to the front elevation.

3. Mark R1, R2 and 1, 2 on the end elevation.

4. Draw circles on the plan of radius R1 and R2. Mark distances 1 and 2 each side of the plan centre line to intersect its corresponding circle. Project these points vertically to intersect their corresponding horizontal lines of the elevation. A curve drawn through these points is the curve of intersection. The same procedure may be used to obtain the curve at the top.

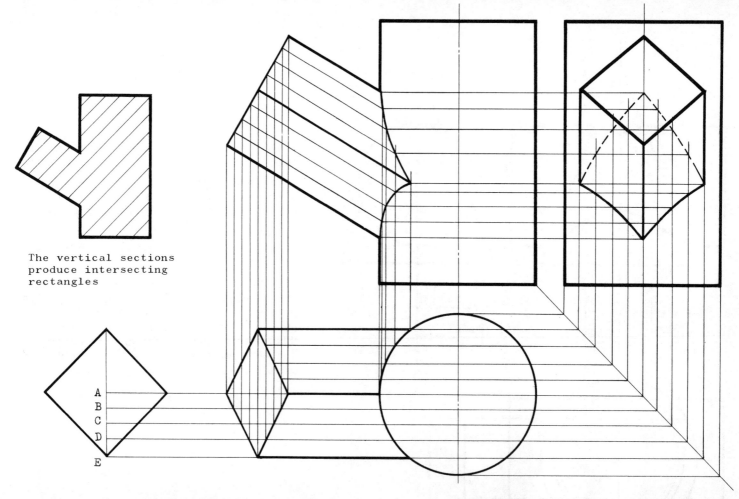

The vertical sections
produce intersecting
rectangles

To Draw the Curves of Interpenetration of a Square Prism Intersecting a Cylinder

1. Draw the vertical sections A, B, C, D, E. At their intersections with the cylinder plan, project lines vertically upwards. Project the lines from the front elevation of the square prism to intersect the vertical lines, to determine the curve points on the front elevation. The curves on the end elevation are the intersections of the lines from the points on the front elevation curve and the lines from the plan.

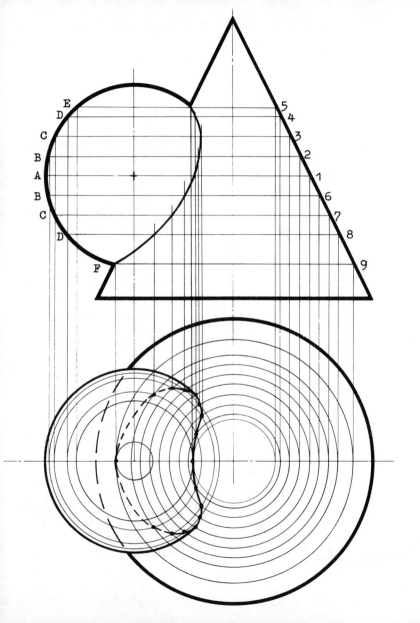

To Draw the Curves of Interpenetration of a Sphere Intersecting a Cone

1. Draw the horizontal section A1 to pass through the centre of the sphere. Take any convenient unit and mark it each side of section A1 to draw the horizontal sections B2, C3, D4, B6, C7, D8. Draw the horizontal sections E5 and F9.

2. Project the points F, D, C, B, A, E, to the centre line of the plan and draw the circular sections. Project the points 9, 8, 7, 6, 1, 2, 3, 4, 5, to the centre line of the plan and draw the circular sections. The intersections of the cone sections with their corresponding sphere sections gives the points for the curve on the plan. Project the points of intersection to their corresponding horizontal sections to obtain the curve points on the front elevation.

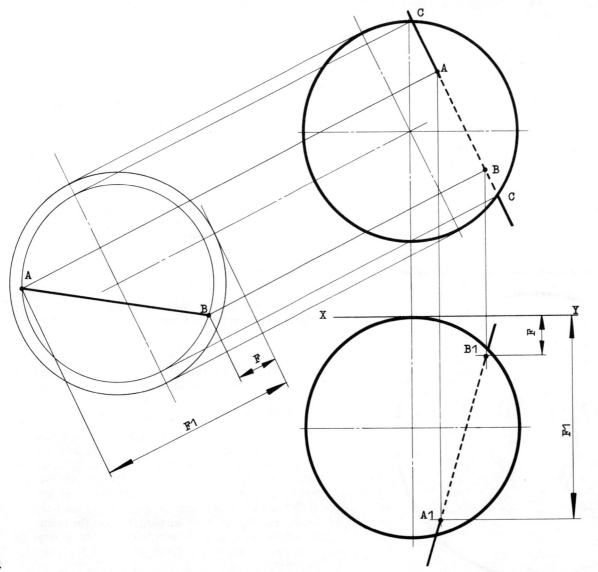

A sphere is pierced by a pin. The pin enters in the front at A and comes out at the rear at B. The positions of A and B are given in the front elevation. To project a plan and find the true length from A to B.

1. Draw the front elevation and the given points A and B.

2. Draw an auxiliary section on the line of the pin CC. Project A and B to the auxiliary section. The section enables the distances (F and F1) in front of the XY line of A1 and B1 in the plan to be found.

3. The distance AB on the auxiliary section is the true length between these points.

Problems of this kind can be solved by taking an auxiliary section on the line of the pin on either the front elevation or the plan.

154

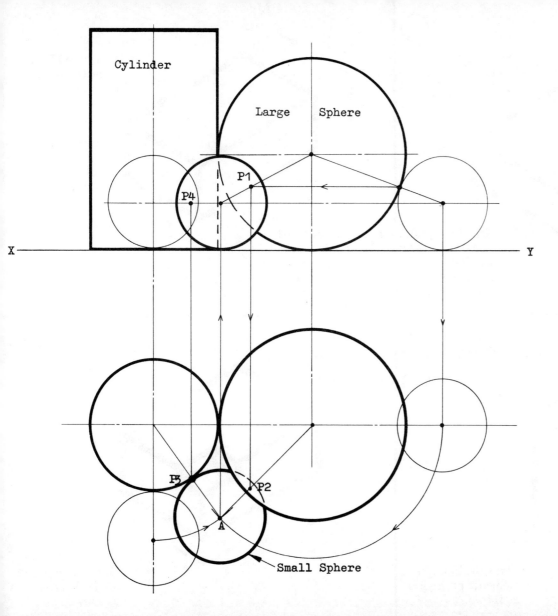

Cylinder

Large   Sphere

P1

P4

X ———————————————————— Y

P3

P2

A

Small Sphere

To Draw Two Spheres and a Cylinder in Contact with Each Other

1. Draw the cylinder and the large sphere in contact in both elevation and plan. The points of contact of these are obvious and are therefore not marked.

2. Draw construction circles of the small sphere in contact with the large circle and the cylinder, and draw the centres of the small sphere to intersect as arcs at A in the plan. The required points of contact, P1, P2, P3, P4, are obtained by the projection shown.

155

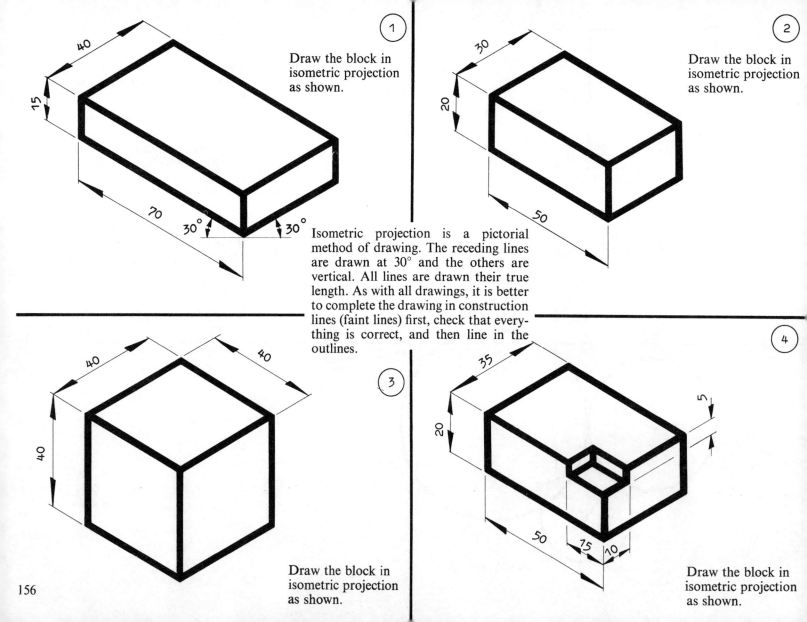

1 Draw the block in isometric projection as shown.

40
15
70
30° 30°

2 Draw the block in isometric projection as shown.

30
20
50

Isometric projection is a pictorial method of drawing. The receding lines are drawn at 30° and the others are vertical. All lines are drawn their true length. As with all drawings, it is better to complete the drawing in construction lines (faint lines) first, check that everything is correct, and then line in the outlines.

3

40
40
40

Draw the block in isometric projection as shown.

4 Draw the block in isometric projection as shown.

35
20
5
50
15
10

156

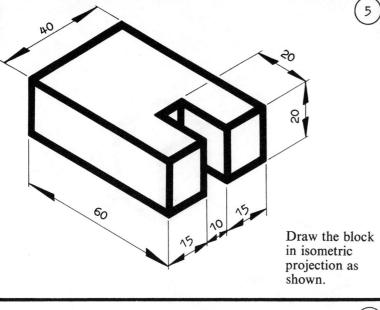

5

Draw the block in isometric projection as shown.

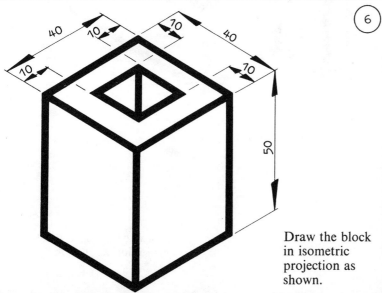

6

Draw the block in isometric projection as shown.

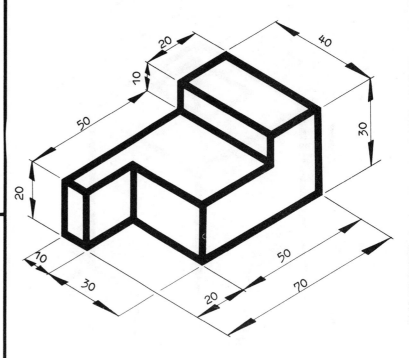

7

Draw the block in isometric projection as shown.

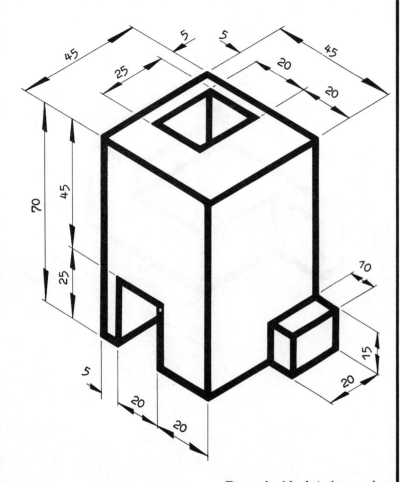

Draw the block in isometric
projection as shown.

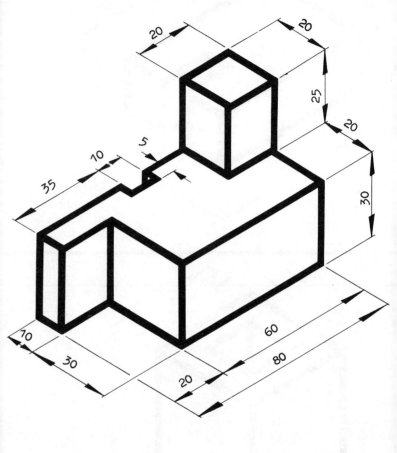

Draw the block in isometric
projection as shown.

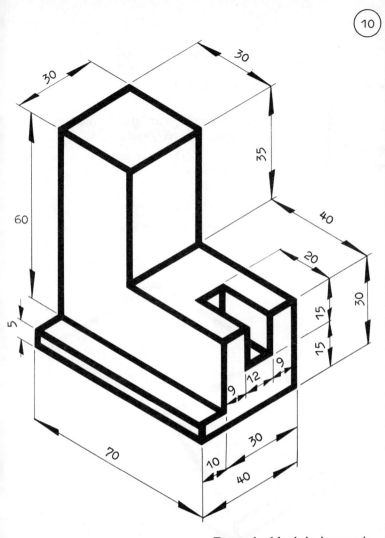

Draw the block in isometric
projection as shown.

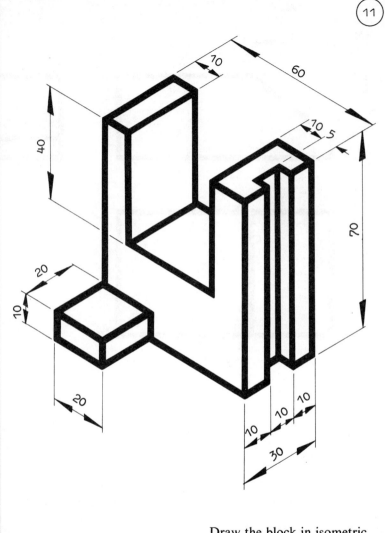

Draw the block in isometric
projection as shown.

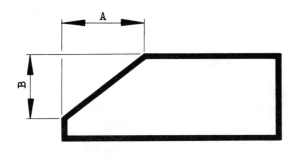

To Make an Isometric Drawing of an Object which is Not Truly Rectangular

Non-rectangular objects must be enclosed in a rectangular box.

1. Draw the isometric box to the dimensions shown in the orthographic drawing.

2. Mark the offsets A and B.

3. Draw the non-isometric lines 1–2, 3–4.

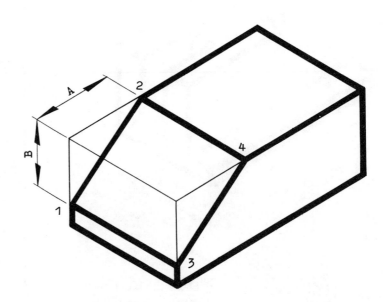

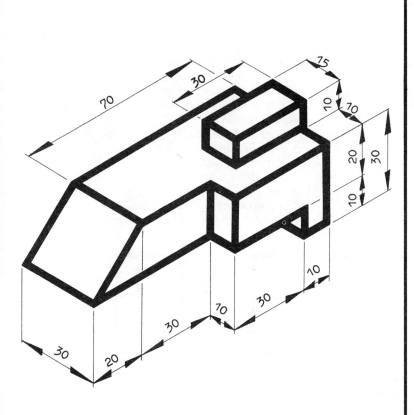

Draw the block in isometric projection as shown.

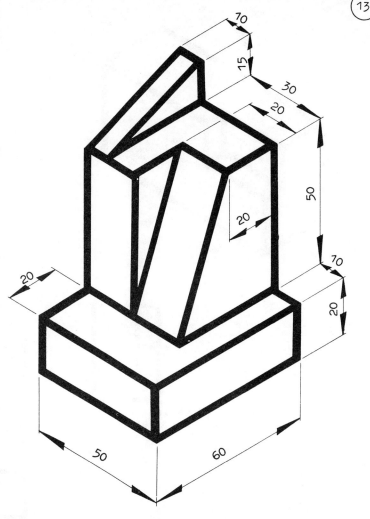

Draw the block in isometric projection as shown.

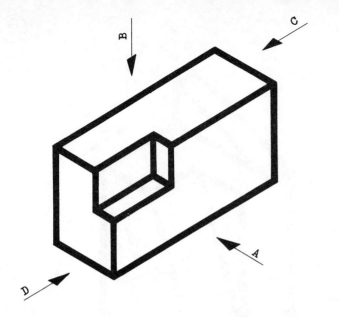

FIRST ANGLE PROJECTION

First angle projection (first angle projection and third angle projection come under the heading of orthographic projection) is a method of drawing an object by means of plane views.

The front elevation is the main view, obtained by looking at the object in the direction of arrow A.

The plan is the view obtained by looking vertically down on the object in the direction of arrow B and placing the view beneath the front elevation and in line with it.

An end elevation is obtained by looking in the direction of the given arrow, and then carrying the view across the front elevation and placing it by the end opposite to that looked at.

Hidden detail is shown by short dashes.

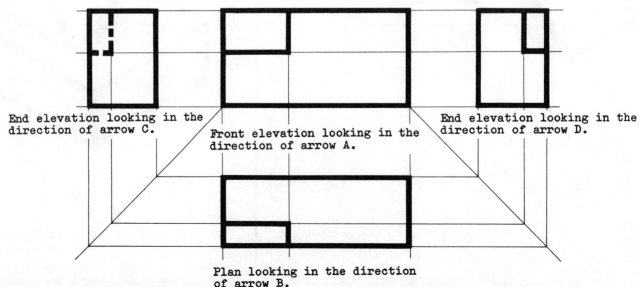

End elevation looking in the direction of arrow C.

Front elevation looking in the direction of arrow A.

End elevation looking in the direction of arrow D.

Plan looking in the direction of arrow B.

162

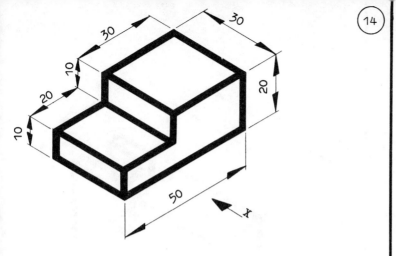

(14)

Draw the block in first angle projection; with the front elevation looking in the direction of arrow X.

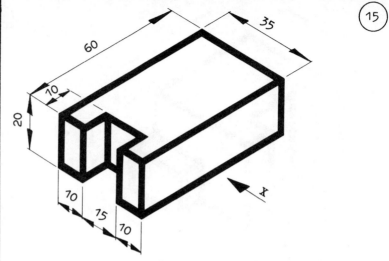

(15)

Draw the block in first angle projection; with the front elevation looking in the direction of arrow X.

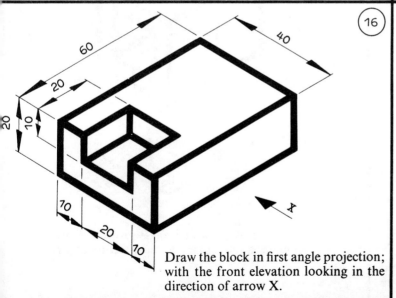

(16)

Draw the block in first angle projection; with the front elevation looking in the direction of arrow X.

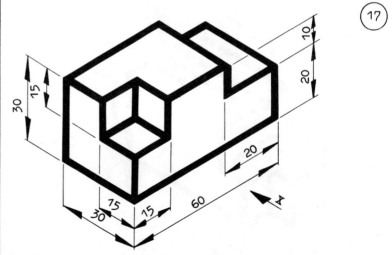

(17)

Draw the block in first angle projection; with the front elevation looking in the direction of arrow X.

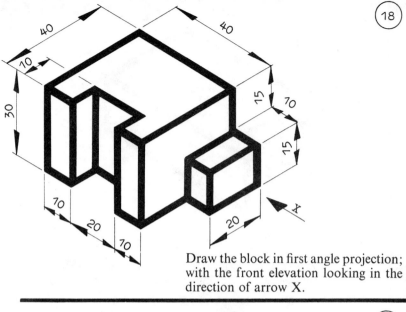

Draw the block in first angle projection; with the front elevation looking in the direction of arrow X.

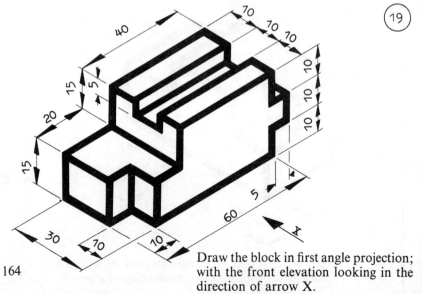

Draw the block in first angle projection; with the front elevation looking in the direction of arrow X.

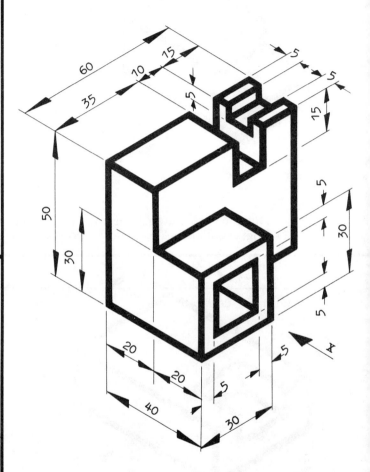

Draw the block in first angle projection; with the front elevation looking in the direction of arrow X.

164

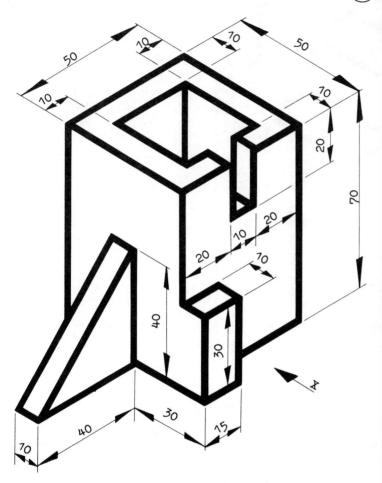

Draw the block in first angle projection; with the front elevation looking in the direction of arrow X.

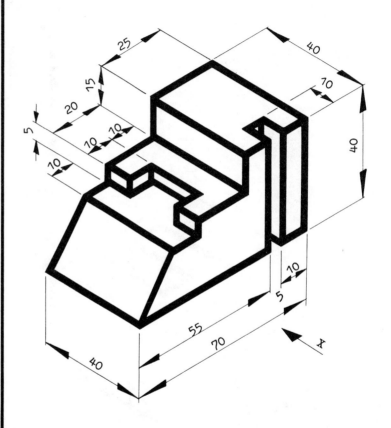

Draw the block in first angle projection; with the front elevation looking in the direction of arrow X.

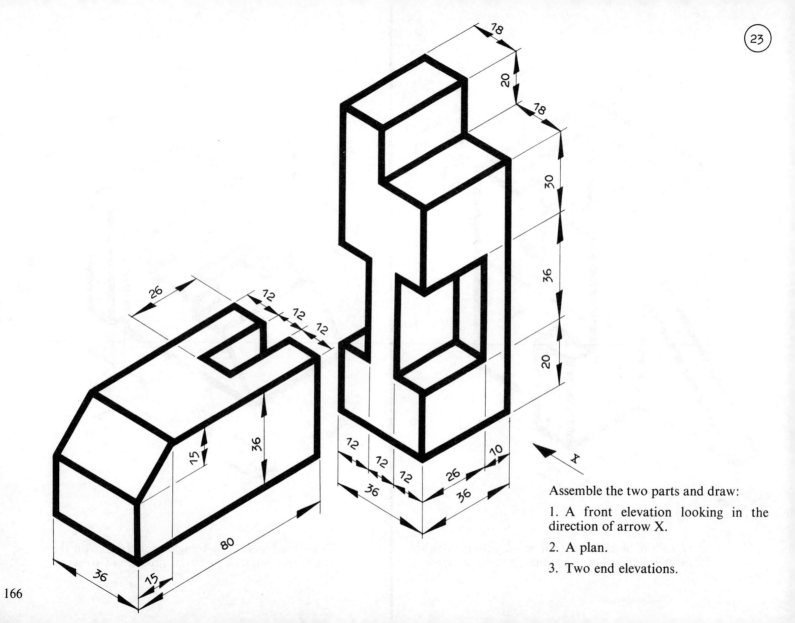

Assemble the two parts and draw:

1. A front elevation looking in the direction of arrow X.

2. A plan.

3. Two end elevations.

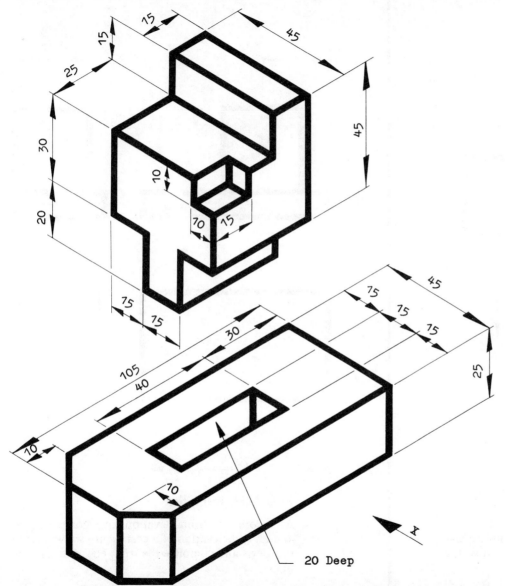

15
25
15
15
45
30
20
45
10
10
15
75
15

45
75
15
15
30
105
40
25
10
10

20 Deep

X

Assemble the two parts and draw:

1. A front elevation looking in the direction of arrow X.

2 A plan.

3. Two end elevations.

167

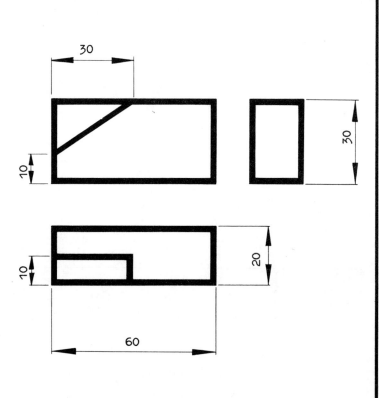

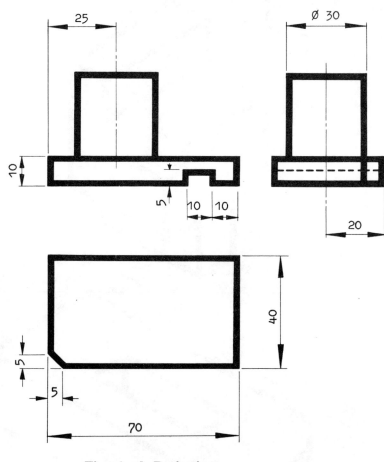

First Angle Projection

A front elevation, a plan, and an incomplete end elevation of a block of wood are shown. Draw the views and complete the end elevation.

First Angle Projection

An incomplete front elevation, an incomplete plan and an end elevation of a casting are shown. Draw the views and complete the front elevation and the plan.

168

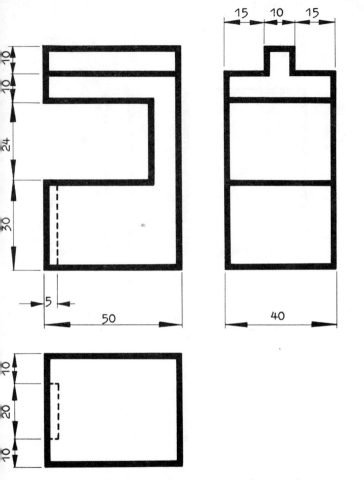

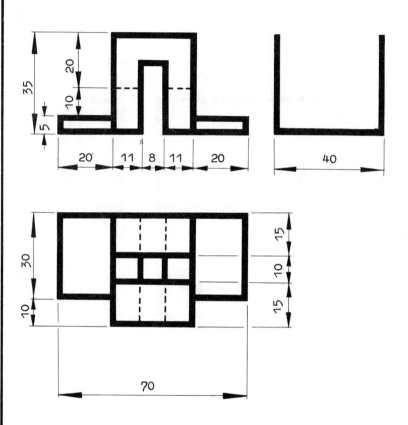

Three views of a block are shown in first angle projection. The end elevation and the plan are incomplete. Draw the three views and complete the end elevation and the plan.

Make an isometric drawing of the block.

A front elevation, a plan, and an incomplete end elevation of a casting are shown in first angle projection. Draw the views and complete the end elevation.

Make an isometric drawing of the casting.

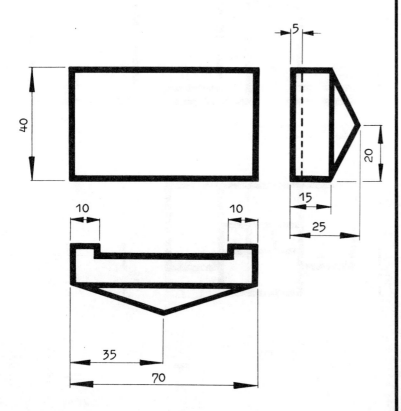

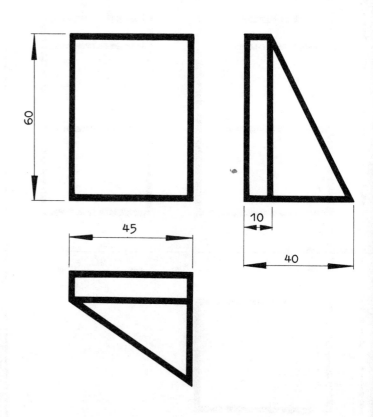

An incomplete front elevation, a plan, and an end elevation of a solid block of wood are shown. Draw these views and complete the front elevation.

An incomplete front elevation, a plan, and an end elevation of a solid block of wood are shown. Draw these views and complete the front elevation.

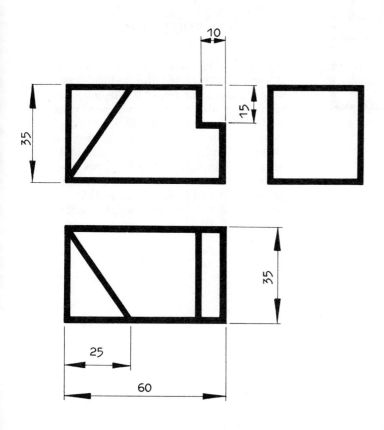

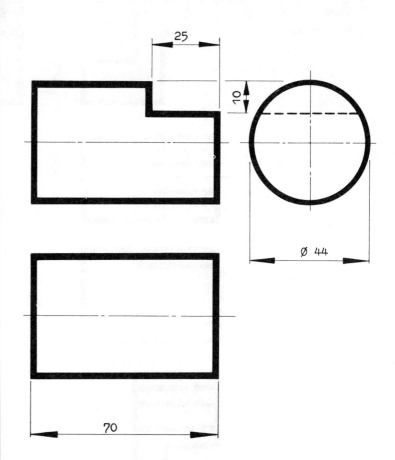

A front elevation, a plan, and an incomplete end elevation of a block of wood is shown. Draw the views and complete the end elevation.

Make an isometric drawing of the block.

A front elevation, an end elevation, and an incomplete plan of a cylinder are shown. Draw the views and complete the plan.

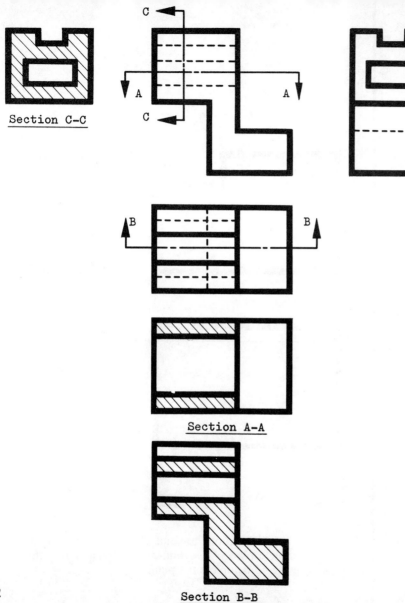

Section C-C

Section A-A

Section B-B

SECTIONS

Hidden details are shown by lines of short dashes, but a clearer way of showing hidden detail is by drawing sections. The object is imagined, to be cut through by a flat sheet of perspex, called the 'cutting plane' (a cutting plane is indicated by a heavy centre line and arrows as shown), and the part behind the plane removed. We now look at the object in the direction of the arrows and draw the view (the section). The actual material cut by the plane is hatched in with lines at 45°.

Hidden detail is not usually shown on sectional views.

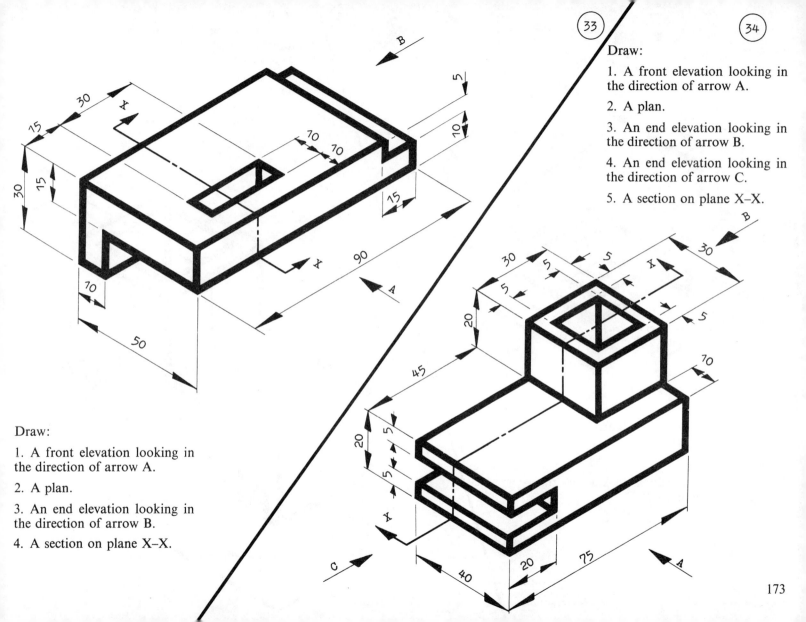

Draw:

1. A front elevation looking in the direction of arrow A.

2. A plan.

3. An end elevation looking in the direction of arrow B.

4. An end elevation looking in the direction of arrow C.

5. A section on plane X–X.

Draw:

1. A front elevation looking in the direction of arrow A.

2. A plan.

3. An end elevation looking in the direction of arrow B.

4. A section on plane X–X.

173

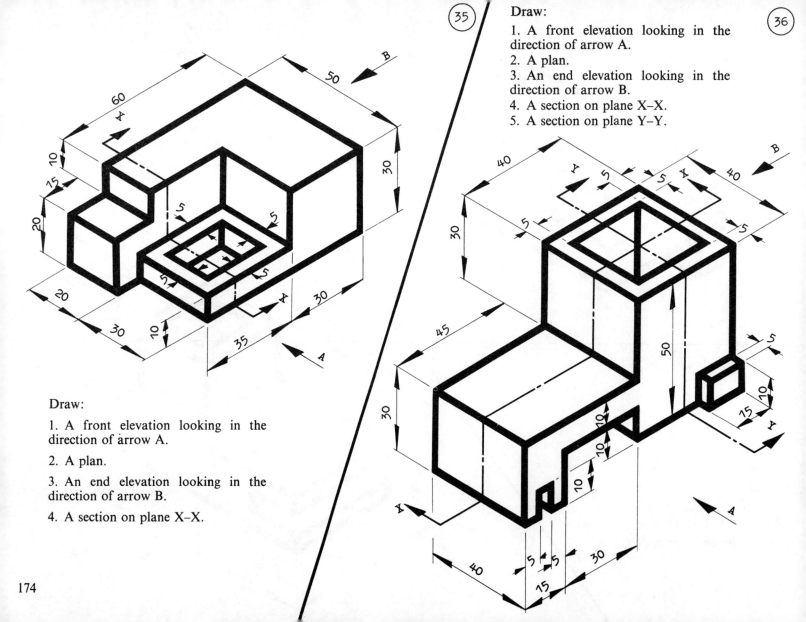

Draw:

1. A front elevation looking in the direction of arrow A.
2. A plan.
3. An end elevation looking in the direction of arrow B.
4. A section on plane X–X.
5. A section on plane Y–Y.

Draw:

1. A front elevation looking in the direction of arrow A.

2. A plan.

3. An end elevation looking in the direction of arrow B.

4. A section on plane X–X.

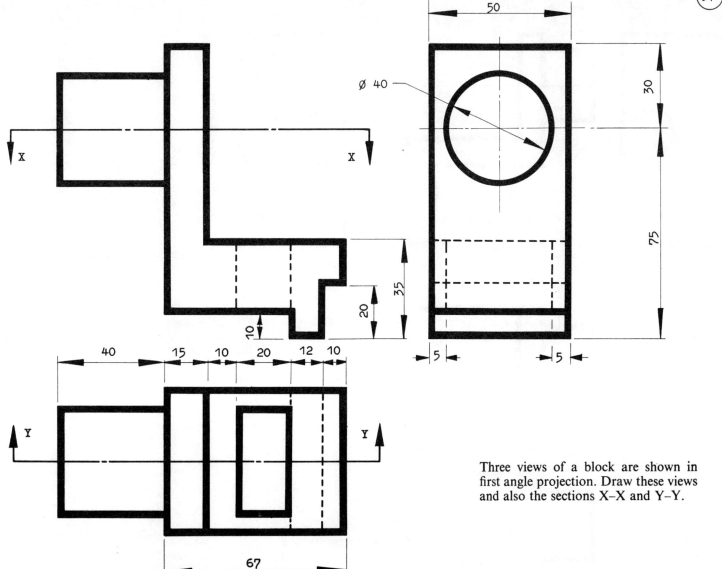

∅ 40

50

30

75

5

5

X

X

Y

Y

40   15   10   20   12   10

35

20

10

67

Three views of a block are shown in first angle projection. Draw these views and also the sections X–X and Y–Y.

175

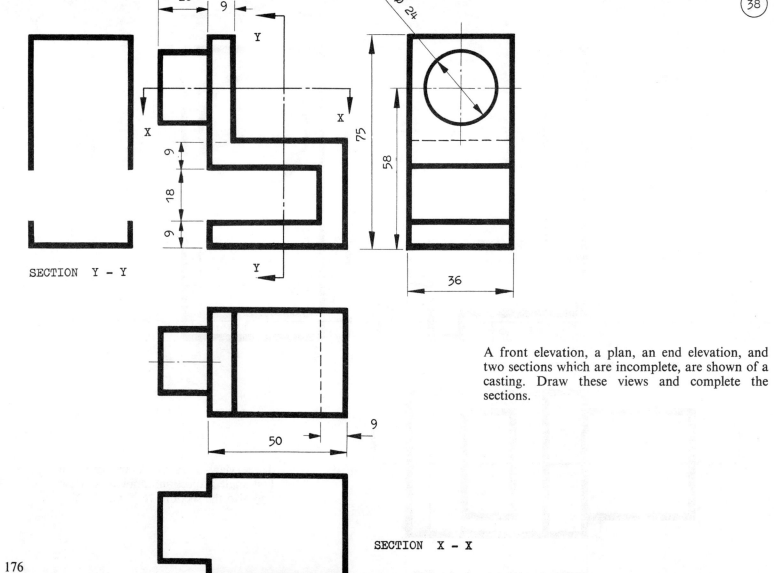

SECTION Y - Y

SECTION X - X

A front elevation, a plan, an end elevation, and two sections which are incomplete, are shown of a casting. Draw these views and complete the sections.

176

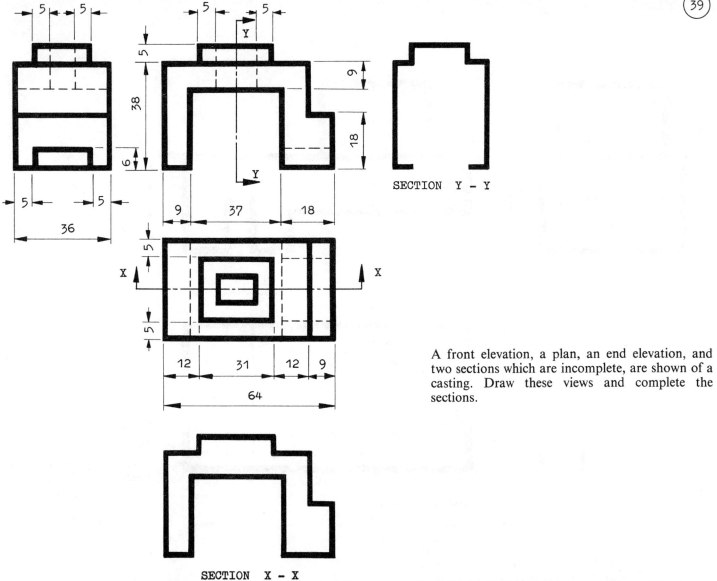

SECTION Y - Y

A front elevation, a plan, an end elevation, and two sections which are incomplete, are shown of a casting. Draw these views and complete the sections.

SECTION X - X

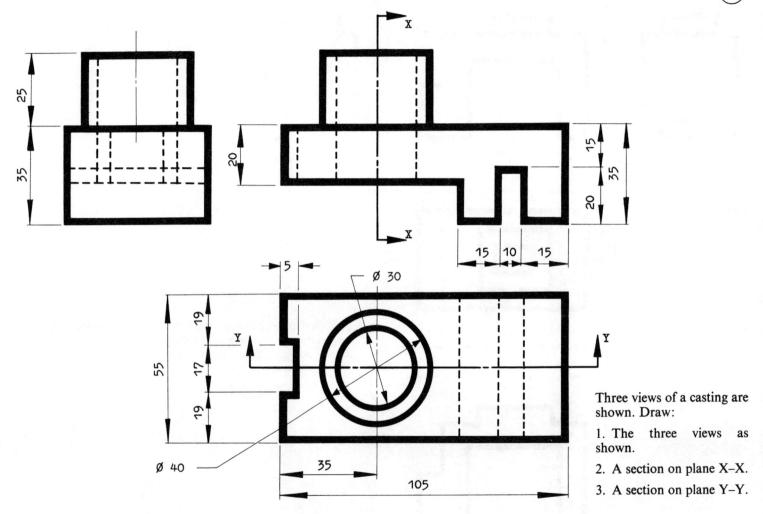

25

35

20

15

35

20

15 10 15

5

Ø 30

Ø 40

19

17

19

55

Y

Y

35

105

X

X

Three views of a casting are shown. Draw:

1. The three views as shown.

2. A section on plane X–X.

3. A section on plane Y–Y.

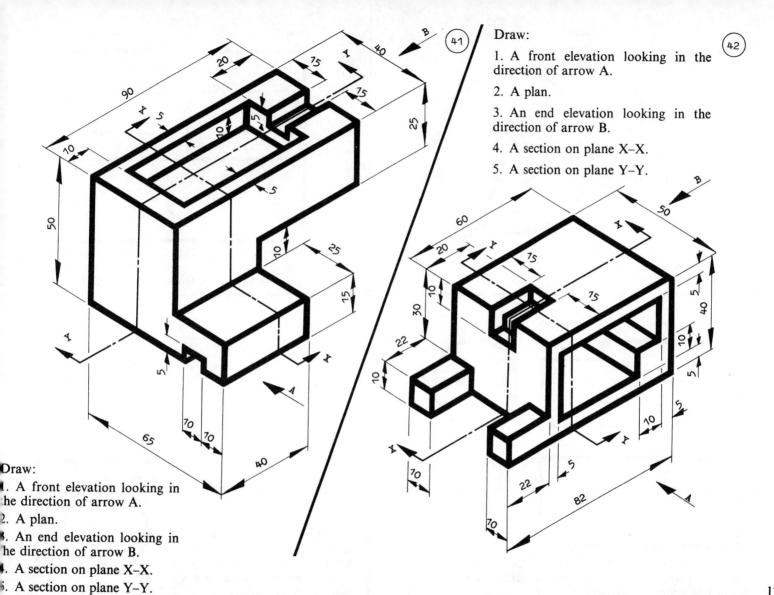

41

42

Draw:

1. A front elevation looking in the direction of arrow A.

2. A plan.

3. An end elevation looking in the direction of arrow B.

4. A section on plane X–X.

5. A section on plane Y–Y.

Draw:

1. A front elevation looking in the direction of arrow A.

2. A plan.

3. An end elevation looking in the direction of arrow B.

4. A section on plane X–X.

5. A section on plane Y–Y.

179

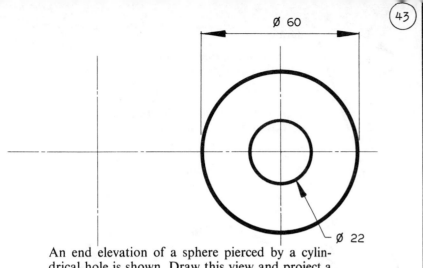

43

Ø 60

Ø 22

An end elevation of a sphere pierced by a cylindrical hole is shown. Draw this view and project a front elevation.

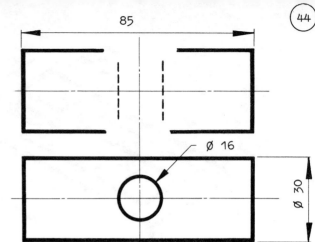

44

85

Ø 16

Ø 30

A cylinder is pierced by a cylindrical hole. An incomplete front elevation, and a plan of this are shown. Draw the two views, and complete the front elevation freehand.

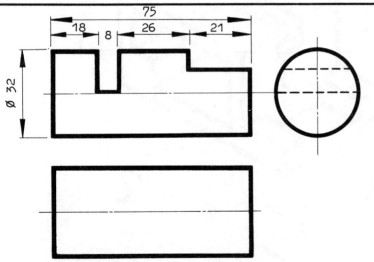

45

75

18 8 26 21

Ø 32

A front elevation, an end elevation, and an incomplete plan, are shown of a cylinder. Draw these views and complete the plan.

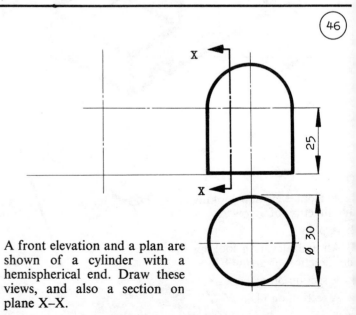

46

X

X

25

Ø 30

A front elevation and a plan are shown of a cylinder with a hemispherical end. Draw these views, and also a section on plane X–X.

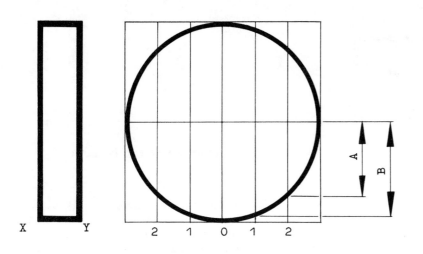

ISOMETRIC PROJECTION OF CIRCLES

To Draw a Circular Disc in Isometric Projection

1. Draw the disc in orthographic projection and enclose the elevation with a square.

2. Divide the horizontal diameter into any number of equal parts and draw vertical lines (0, 1, 2) through the ordinates.

3. Draw the square enclosing the disc in isometric projection and transfer lines, 0, 1, 2 to it.

4. Transfer the horizontal diameter to the isometric square and mark A and B each side of it. Draw a curve through the intersection of 1B and 2A.

5. Draw perpendiculars from the intersections and mark the thickness of the disc (XY).

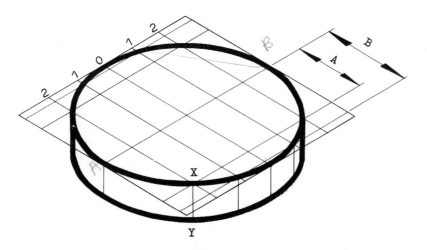

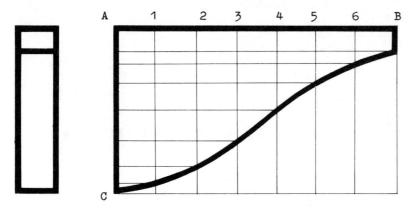

·Fig. 1

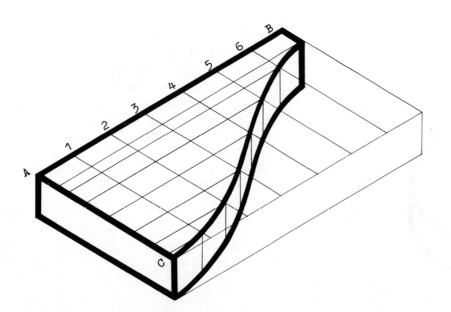

To Draw a Curve in Isometric Projection

1. Enclose the curve (fig. 1) with a rectangle and divide AB into any number of equal parts. Draw lines from these ordinates perpendicular to AB.

2. Draw the rectangular block in isometric projection and divide AB into the same number of equal parts as previously. Transfer the ordinates from AC on the orthographic view. Draw a curve through the intersection of the lines.

3. To draw the curve on the lower face, drop verticals from the curve and mark the thickness on them.

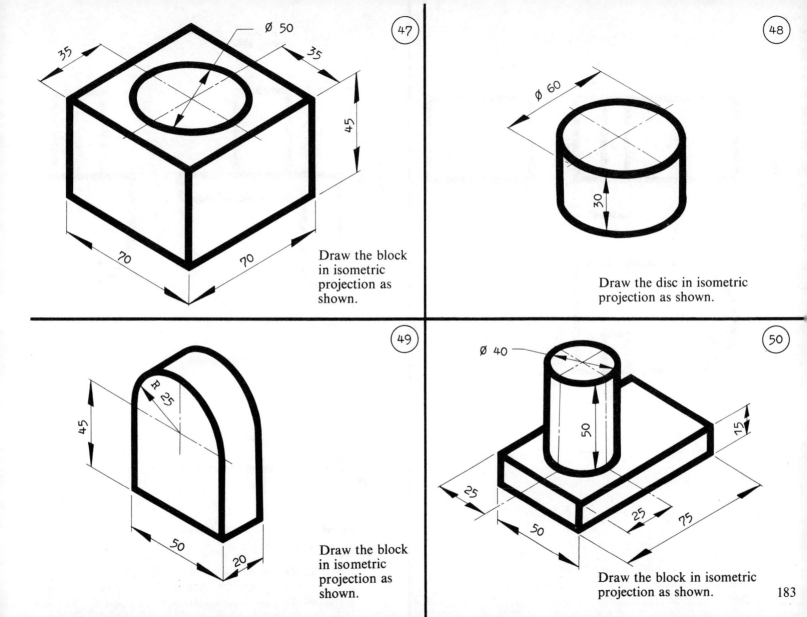

(47) Ø 50
35
35
45
70
70
Draw the block in isometric projection as shown.

(48) Ø 60
30
Draw the disc in isometric projection as shown.

(49) R 25
45
50
20
Draw the block in isometric projection as shown.

(50) Ø 40
50
25
50
25
75
15
Draw the block in isometric projection as shown.

183

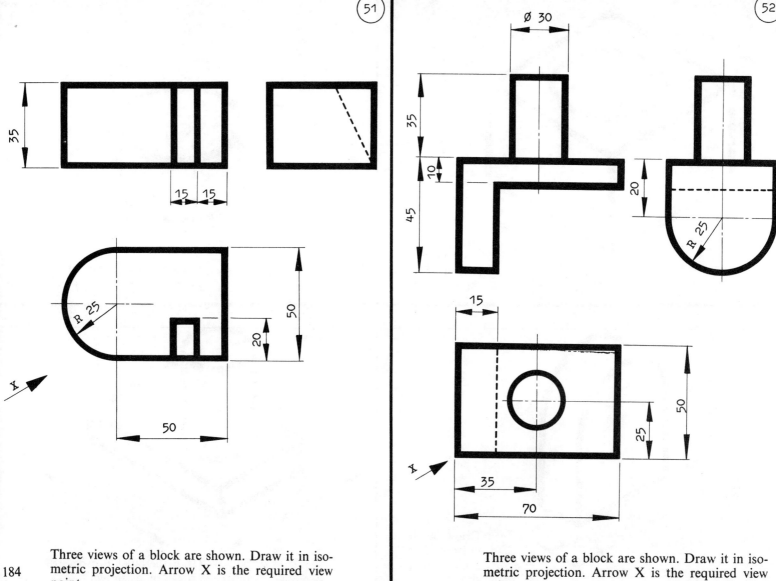

Three views of a block are shown. Draw it in isometric projection. Arrow X is the required view
point.

Three views of a block are shown. Draw it in isometric projection. Arrow X is the required view
point.

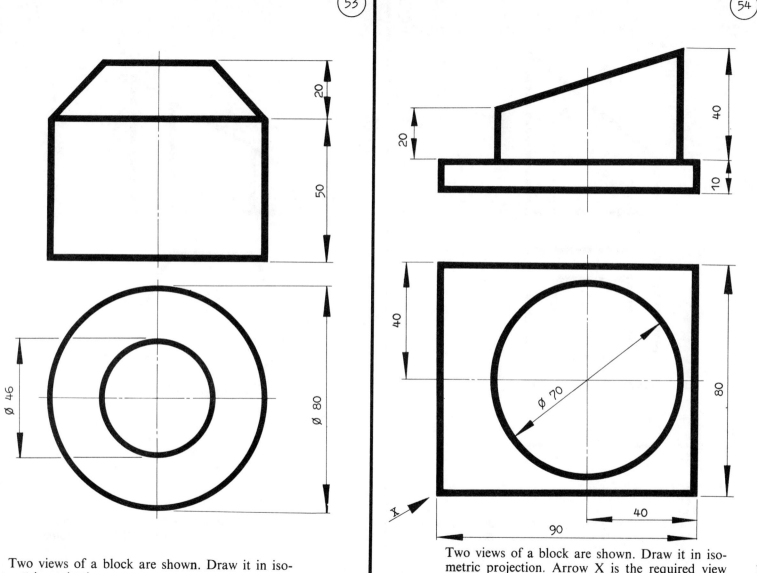

Two views of a block are shown. Draw it in isometric projection.

Two views of a block are shown. Draw it in isometric projection. Arrow X is the required view
point.

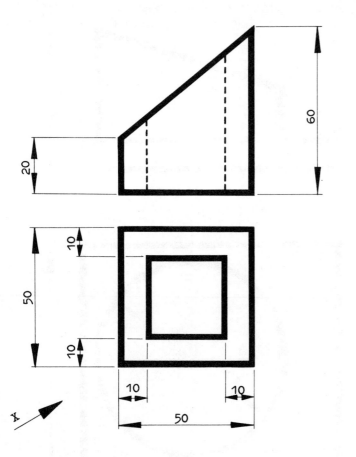

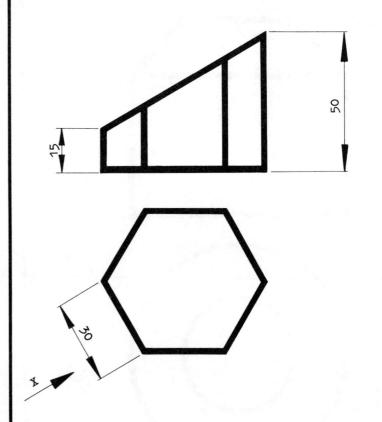

Two views of a block are shown. Draw this in iso-metric projection. Arrow X is the required view point.

Two views of a block are shown. Draw this in isometric projection. Arrow X is the required view point.

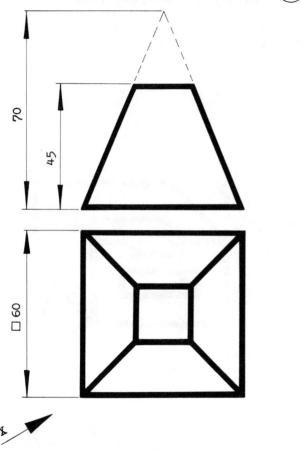

Two views of a frustum of a square pyramid are shown. Draw this in isometric projection. Arrow X is the required view point.

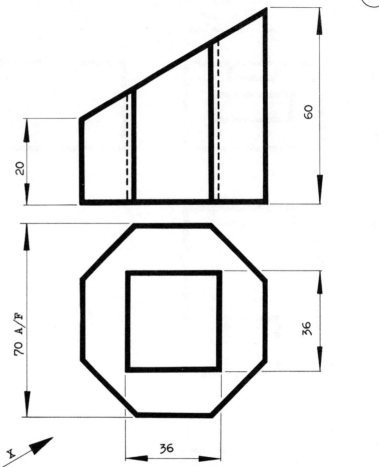

Two views of a frustum of a regular octagonal prism, which is pierced by a square hole, are shown. Draw this in isometric projection. Arrow X is the required view point.

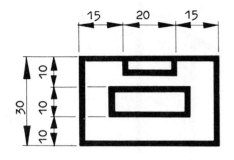

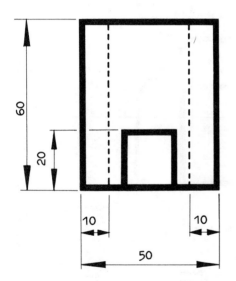

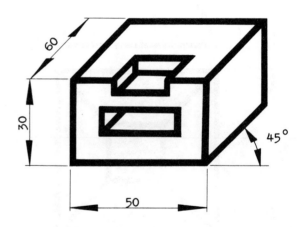

Oblique projection is a pictorial method. The object is viewed at right angles to one face. The receding (oblique) lines may be drawn at any angle, but 45°, 30° or 60° set-square angles are usually used for convenience. The oblique lines are usually drawn half-size (but dimensioned full-size) to prevent distortion of the drawing.

Circles and curves are drawn by the same method as shown on pages 181 and 182.

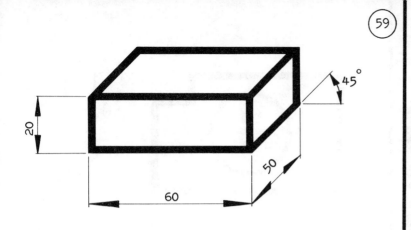

(59)

45°

20

50

60

Draw the block in oblique projection as shown.

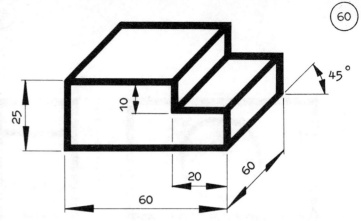

(60)

45°

25

10

20

60

60

Draw the block in oblique projection as shown.

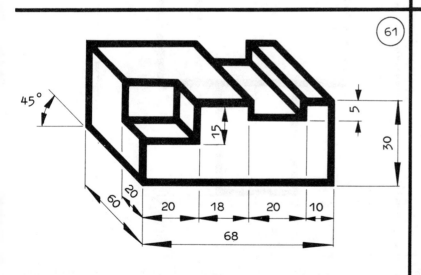

(61)

45°

15

5

30

60

20

20

18

20

10

68

Draw the block in oblique projection as shown.

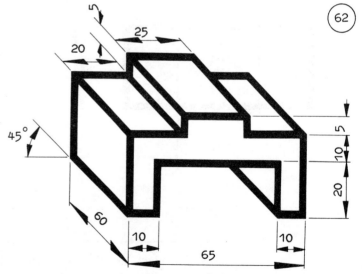

(62)

5

25

20

45°

5

10

20

60

10

65

10

Draw the block in oblique projection as shown.

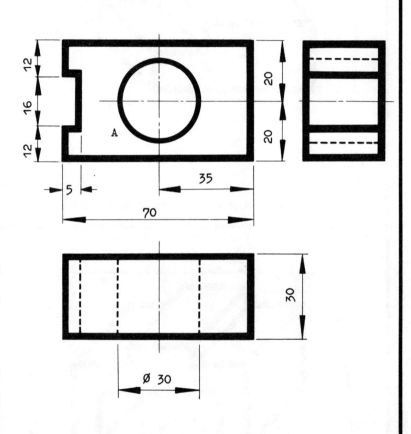

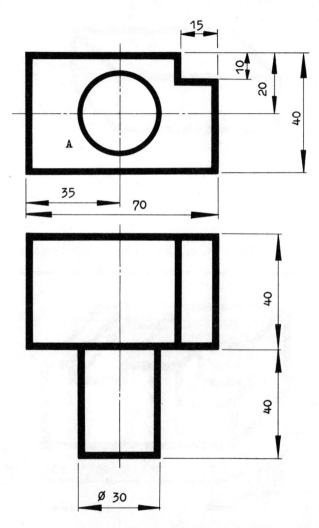

Three views of a block are shown. Draw it in oblique projection, with face A parallel to the plane of projection.

Two views of a block are shown. Draw it in oblique projection, with face A parallel to the plane of projection.

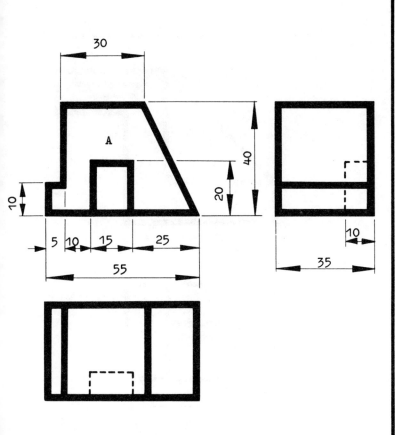

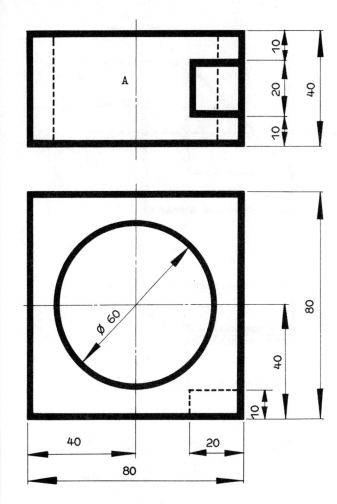

Three views of a block are shown. Draw it in oblique projection, with face A parallel to the plane of projection.

Two views of a block are shown. Draw it in oblique projection, with face A parallel to the plane of projection.

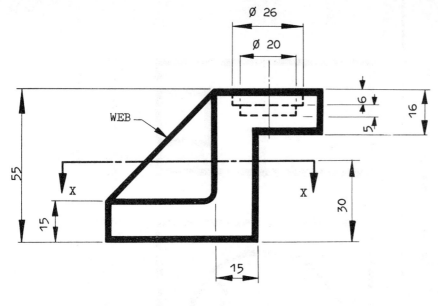

WEB

Ø 26

Ø 20

16

6

5

55

15

30

15

X   X

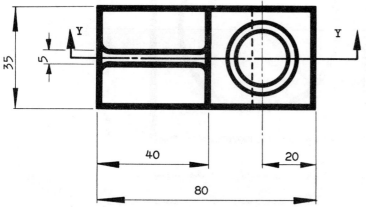

Y   Y

35

5

40   20

80

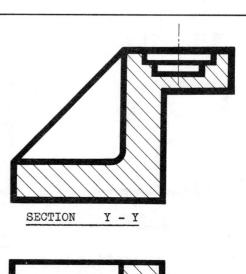

SECTION   Y - Y

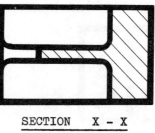

SECTION   X - X

This is the solution to the exercise. Note that we do not section webs in the front elevation.

A front elevation and a plan, in first angle projection, are shown of a casting. Draw:

1. A front elevation and a plan as shown.

2. A section on plane X–X.

3. A section on plane Y–Y.

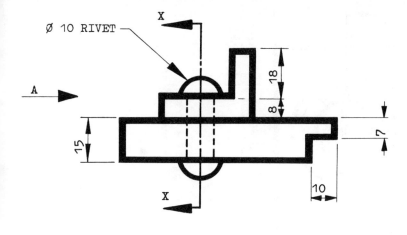

Ø 10 RIVET

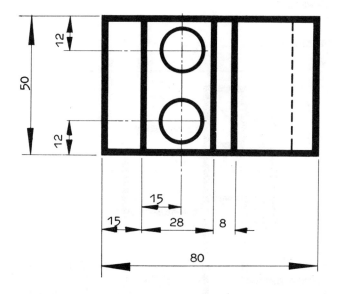

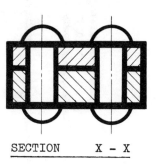

SECTION   X – X

This is the solution to the exercise. Note that we do not section rivets.

A front elevation and a plan, in first angle projection, are shown of two plates riveted together. Draw:
1. The two views shown.
2. An end elevation looking in the direction of arrow A.
3. A section on plane X–X.

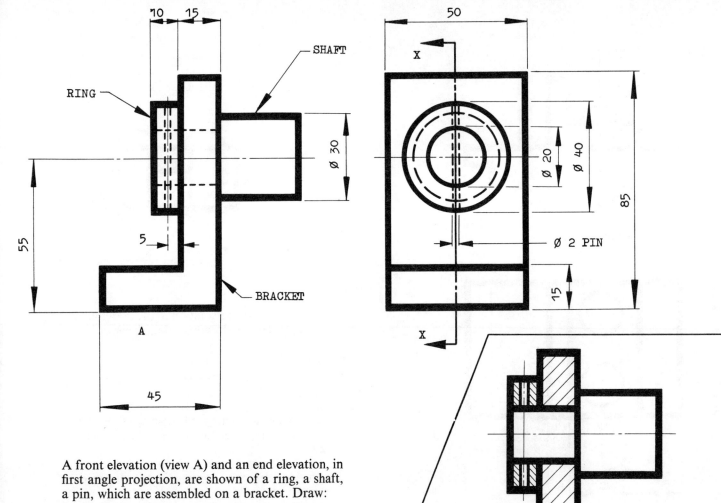

A front elevation (view A) and an end elevation, in first angle projection, are shown of a ring, a shaft, a pin, which are assembled on a bracket. Draw:

1. The given views.

2. A plan.

3. A section on plane X–X.

This is the solution to the exercise. Note that we do not section shafts and pins.

SECTION X – X

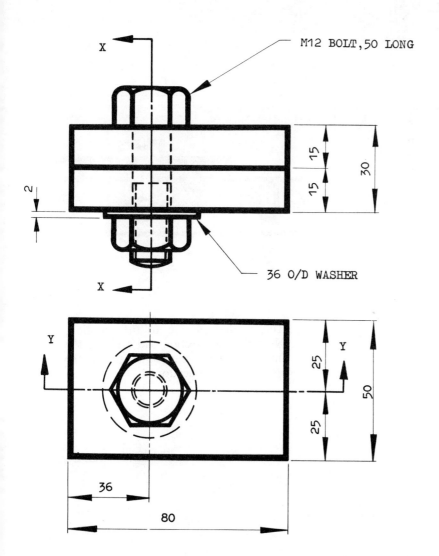

M12 BOLT, 50 LONG

36 O/D WASHER

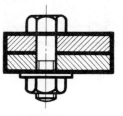

SECTION Y - Y

This is the solution to the exercise. Note that we do not section bolts, nuts, and washers; and also that adjacent pieces are hatched opposite ways.

Two metal plates are bolted together as shown. Draw the two given views, and also a section on plane X–X and a section on plane Y–Y.

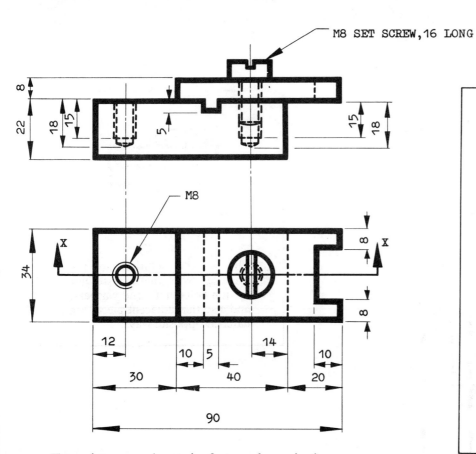

M8 SET SCREW, 16 LONG

M8

X

X

Two views are shown in first angle projection. Draw the given views, and add an end elevation and a section on plane X–X.

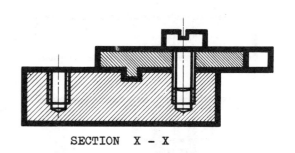

SECTION X – X

This is the solution to the question. Note that we section the walls of the internal screw thread; and also that the set screw is not sectioned.

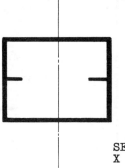

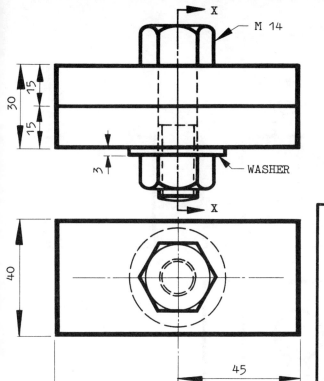

M 14

WASHER

X

SECTION
X - X

First Angle Projection

Draw the front elevation and the plan
and complete the section X–X.
  Supply the missing dimensions.

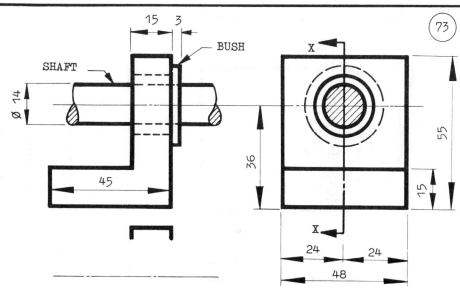

SHAFT

BUSH

Ø 14

15 3

45

36

55

15

24   24

48

First Angle Projection

Draw the front elevation and the end
elevation and complete the section
X–X.
  Supply the missing dimensions.

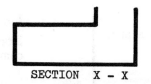

SECTION X - X

72

73

197

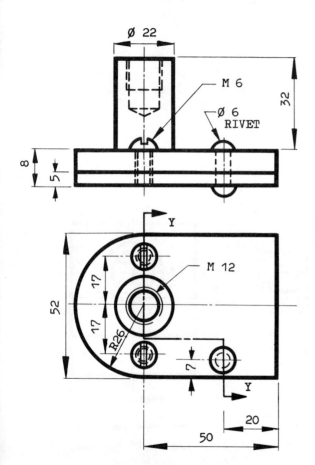

First Angle Projection

Draw:

1. Draw a front elevation and a plan as shown.

2. A section on plane Y–Y.

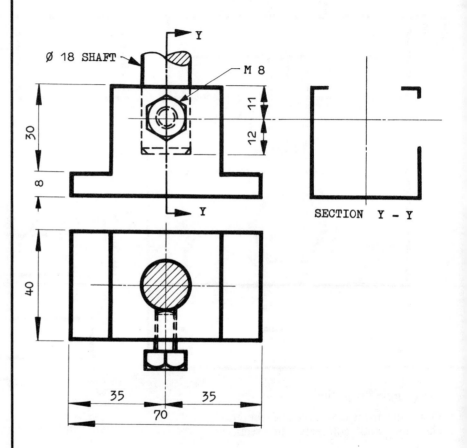

First Angle Projection

Draw the front elevation and plan as shown and complete the section Y–Y.

Supply the missing dimensions.

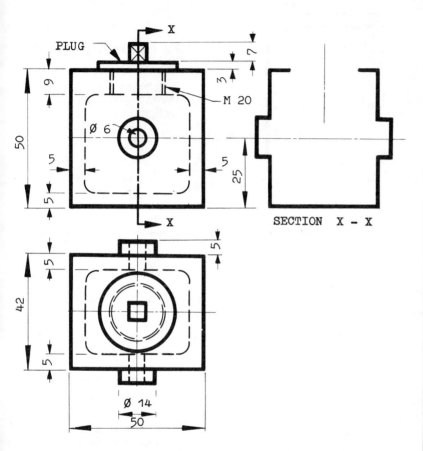

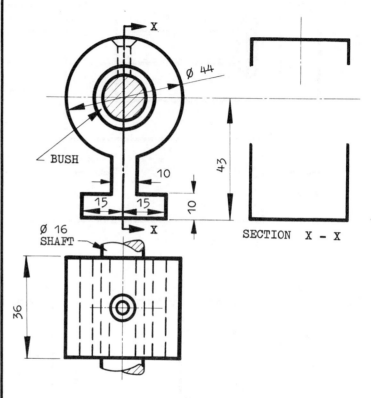

First Angle Projection

Draw the front elevation and plan as shown and
complete the section X–X.

Supply the missing dimensions.

First Angle Projection

Draw the front elevation and the plan as shown
and complete the section X–X.

Supply the missing dimensions.

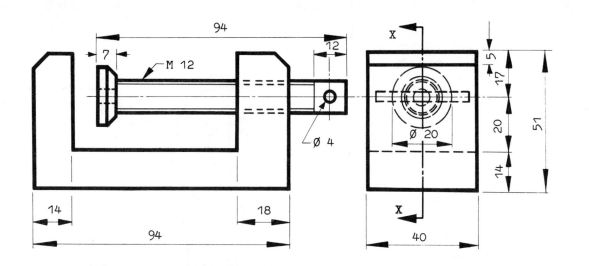

First Angle Projection

Draw the front elevation and the end elevation as shown, and also draw a section on plane X–X.

Supply the missing dimensions.

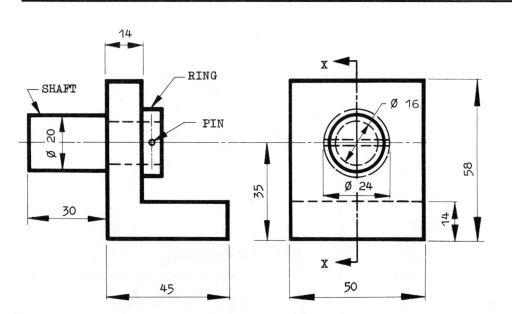

First Angle Projection

Draw the front elevation and the end elevation as shown, and also draw a section on plane X–X.

Supply the missing dimensions.

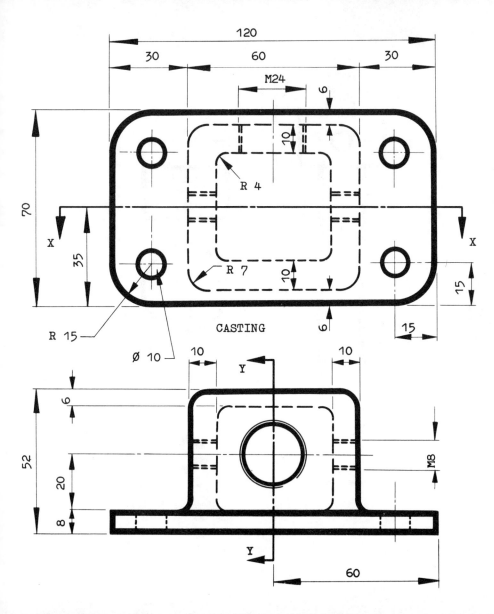

CASTING

120
30
60
30
M24
6
R 4
R 7
70
35
10
15
X
X
10
15
R 15
Ø 10
10
Y
10
6
52
20
8
M8
Y
60

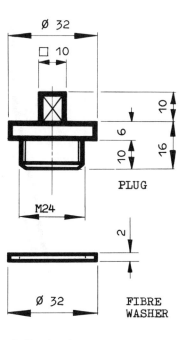

Ø 32
□ 10
10
6
16
10
10
M24
PLUG

2
Ø 32
FIBRE
WASHER

First Angle Projection

Place the plug and the fibre washer in position in the casting and draw:

1. A front elevation.

2. A section on plane X–X.

3. A section on plane Y–Y.

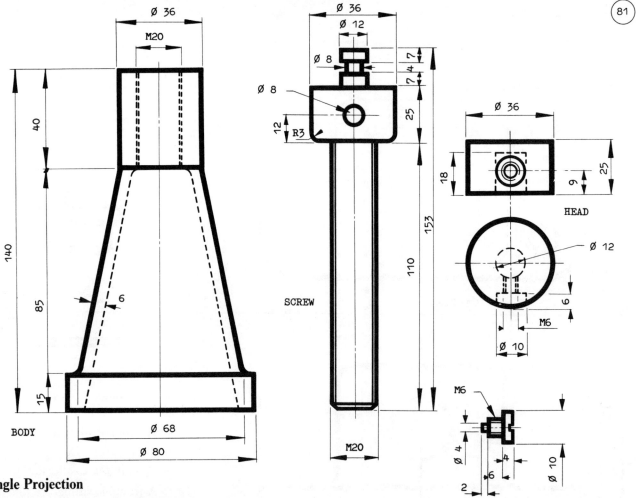

Ø 36
M20
40
140
85
6
15
BODY
Ø 68
Ø 80

Ø 36
Ø 12
Ø 8
7
4
7
Ø 8
12
R3
25
SCREW
153
110
M20

Ø 36
18
25
9
HEAD
Ø 12
6
M6
Ø 10

M6
Ø 4
4
6
Ø 10
2

(81)

First Angle Projection

Details of a bottle jack are shown. Draw the
following views of the jack completely assembled,
with 10 millimetres of the thread showing:
1. A sectional elevation on the vertical centre line.
2. A plan.

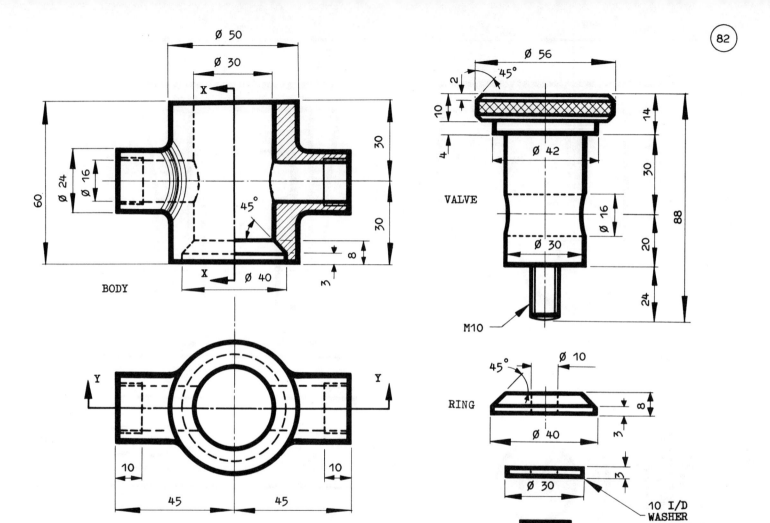

Ø 50

Ø 30

X

30

Ø 24
Ø 16

60

45°

30

X
Ø 40

8

3

BODY

Ø 56

45°

2

10

4

VALVE

Ø 42

14

30

Ø 16

88

Ø 30

20

24

M10

Y
Y

10
10

45
45

RING

45°

Ø 10

8

Ø 40

3

Ø 30

3

10 I/D
WASHER

M10

(82)

First Angle Projection

Details of a stop cock are shown. Assemble the
parts and with the valve in the open position draw
the following views:

1. A section on plane Y–Y.
2. A plan.
3. A section on plane X–X.

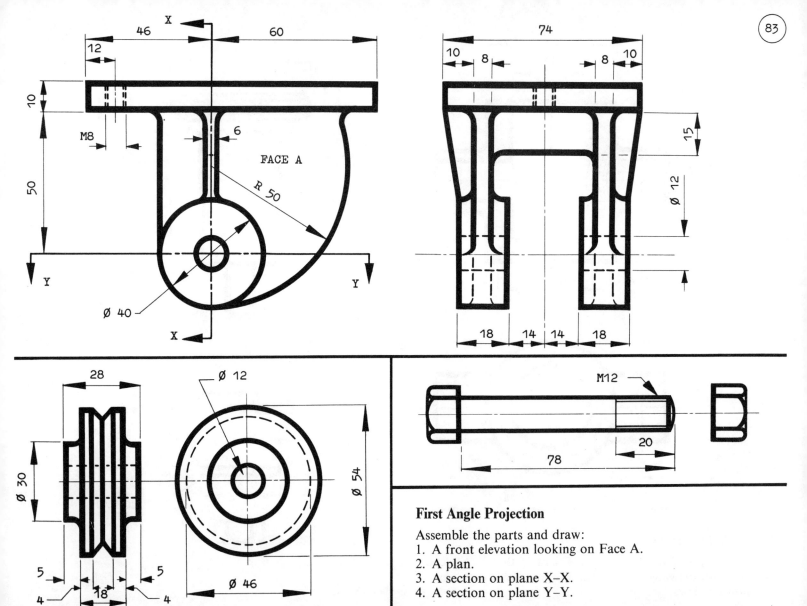

83

X

46

60

12

10

M8

50

FACE A

R 50

Ø 40

Y

Y

X

74

10

8

8

10

15

Ø 12

18

14

14

18

6

28

Ø 12

Ø 30

Ø 54

5

5

4

18

4

Ø 46

M12

20

78

First Angle Projection

Assemble the parts and draw:
1. A front elevation looking on Face A.
2. A plan.
3. A section on plane X–X.
4. A section on plane Y–Y.

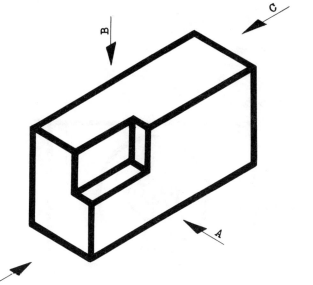

THIRD ANGLE PROJECTION

Third angle projection is a method of drawing an object by means of flat views. The placing of the views is the opposite to first angle projection.

The front elevation is the main view, obtained by looking at the object in the direction of arrow A.

The plan is the view obtained by looking vertically down on to the object in the direction of arrow B and placing the view above the front elevation and in line with it.

An end elevation is obtained by looking in the direction of the given arrow, and then placing the view by the end looked at.

Hidden detail is shown by short dashes.

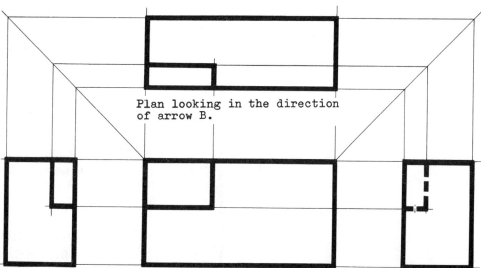

Plan looking in the direction of arrow B.

End elevation looking in the direction of arrow D.

Front elevation looking in the direction of arrow A.

End elevation looking in the direction of arrow C.

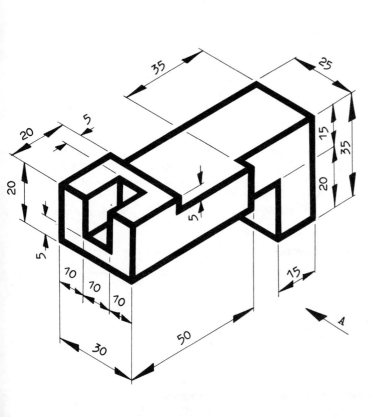

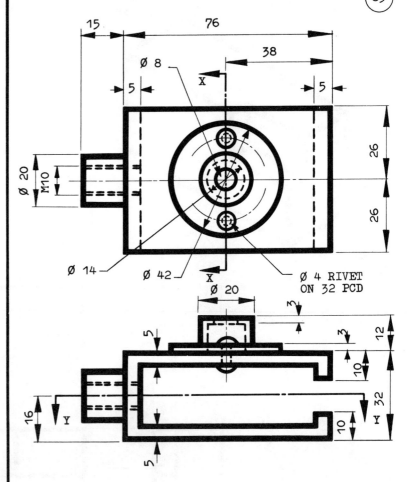

Third Angle Projection

Draw a front elevation and a plan as shown, and add a section on plane X–X and a section on plane Y–Y.

Draw the block in third angle projection, with the front elevation looking in the direction of arrow A.

206

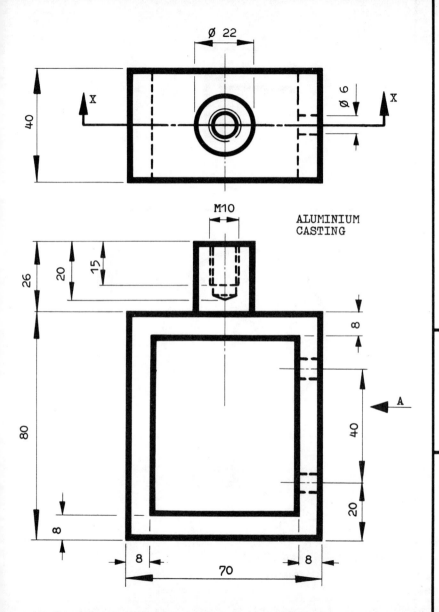

Ø 22

Ø 6

X — X

40

ALUMINIUM
CASTING

M10

26

20

15

8

80

40

20

8

8

70

8

A

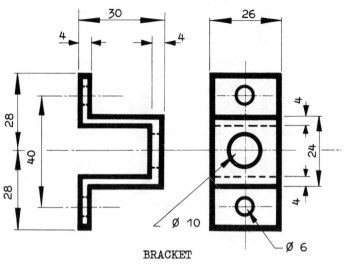

30

4

4

28

40

28

26

4

24

4

Ø 10

Ø 6

BRACKET

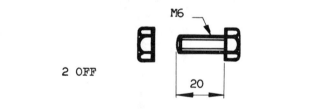

M6

2 OFF

20

Third Angle Projection

Bolt the bracket on the outside of the casting and
draw:
1. A section on plane X–X.
2. A plan.
3. An end elevation looking in the direction of
arrow A.

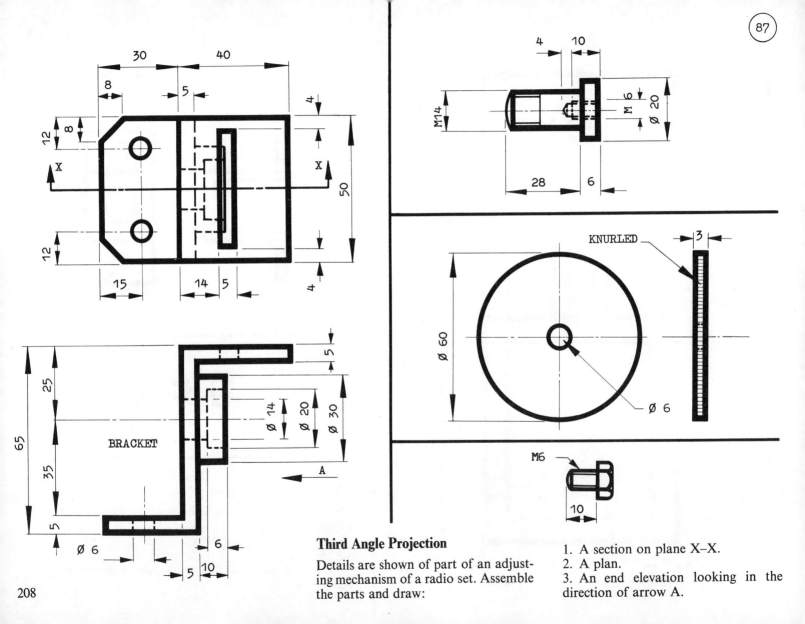

87

30
40
8
5
4
12
8
X
X
50
12
15
14
5
4

4
10
M14
M6
Ø20
M6
28
6

KNURLED
3
Ø60
Ø6

BRACKET
25
5
65
35
14
20
30
Ø
Ø
Ø
A
5
Ø6
6
5
10

M6
10

208

Third Angle Projection

Details are shown of part of an adjusting mechanism of a radio set. Assemble the parts and draw:

1. A section on plane X–X.
2. A plan.
3. An end elevation looking in the direction of arrow A.

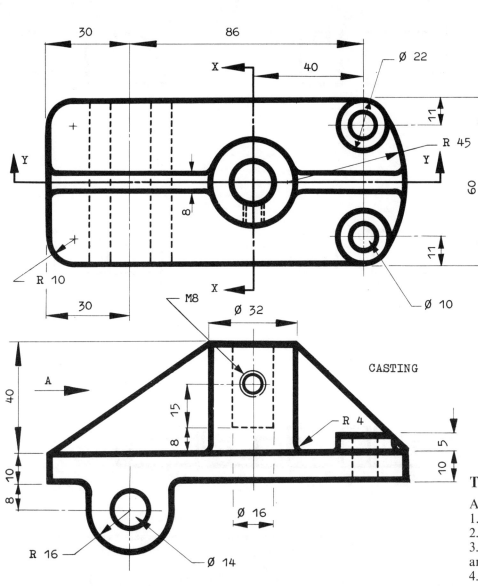

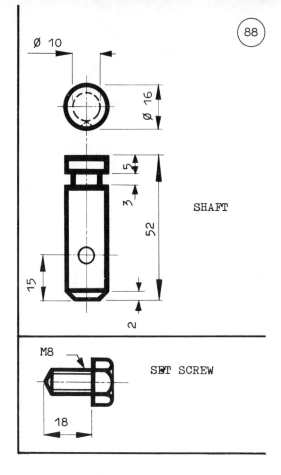

Ø 10

Ø 16

SHAFT

5

3

52

15

2

M8

SET SCREW

18

Ø 22

R 45

Ø 10

M8

Ø 32

CASTING

R 4

Ø 16

R 16

Ø 14

30

86

40

11

X

Y

Y

X

60

11

8

30

R 10

40

A

15

8

10

8

5

10

Third Angle Projection

Assemble the parts and draw:
1. A section on plane Y–Y.
2. A plan.
3. An end elevation looking in the direction of arrow A.
4. A section on plane X–X.

209

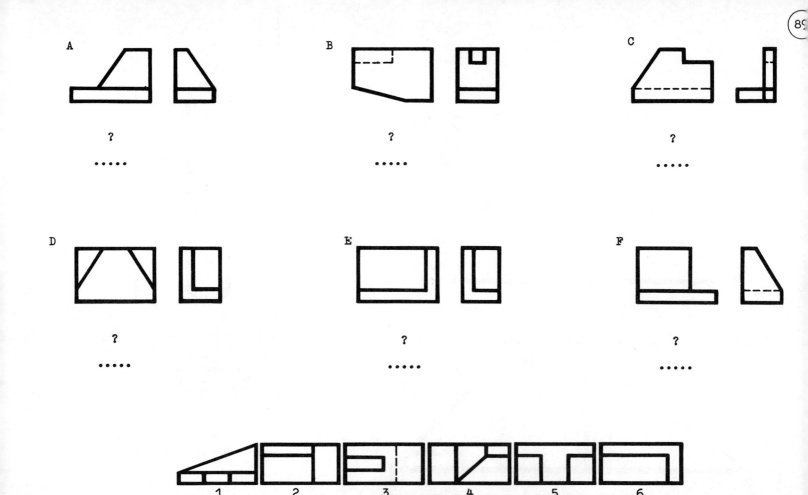

A
?
.....

B
?
.....

C
?
.....

D
?
.....

E
?
.....

F
?
.....

First Angle Projection

From the numbered plans select the correct one to replace each of the question marks.

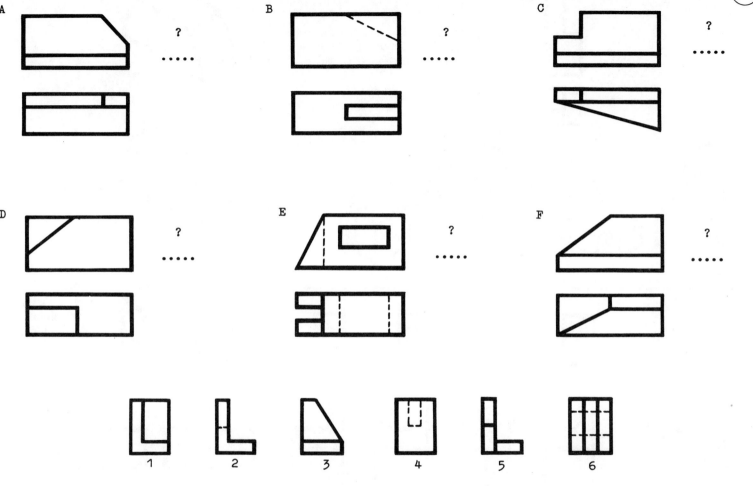

First Angle Projection

From the numbered end views select the correct one to replace each of the question marks.

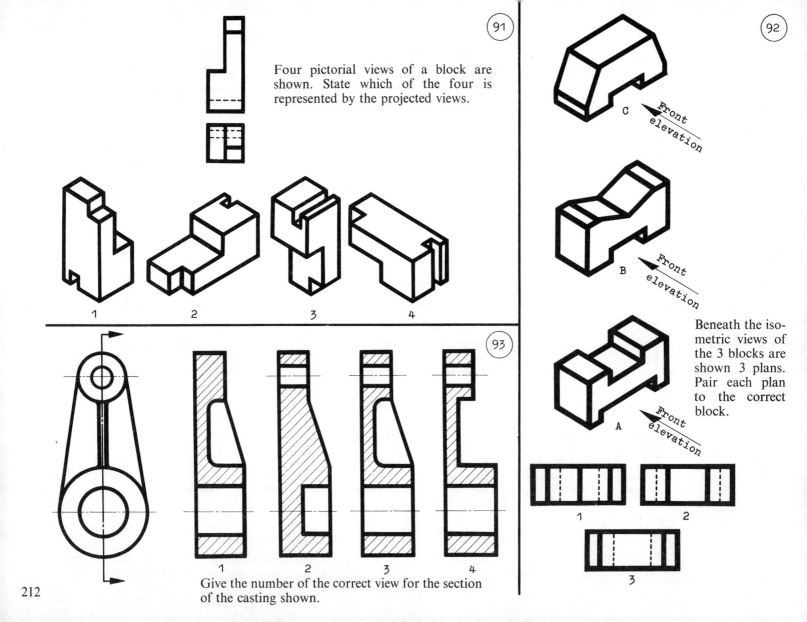

91

Four pictorial views of a block are shown. State which of the four is represented by the projected views.

1   2   3   4

92

C
Front elevation

B
Front elevation

Beneath the isometric views of the 3 blocks are shown 3 plans. Pair each plan to the correct block.

A
Front elevation

1   2

3

93

Give the number of the correct view for the section of the casting shown.

1   2   3   4

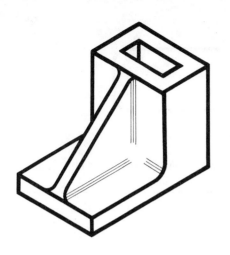

Draw freehand a pictorial view of the casting in isometric projection. Use an isometric grid, or drawing paper.

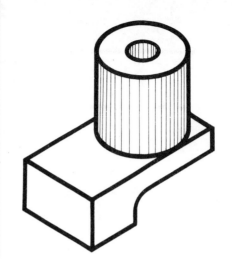

Draw freehand a pictorial view of the casting in isometric projection. Use an isometric grid, or drawing paper.

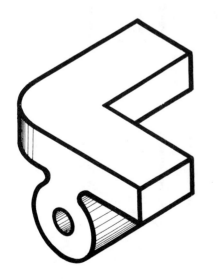

Draw freehand a pictorial view of the casting in isometric projection. Use an isometric grid, or drawing paper.

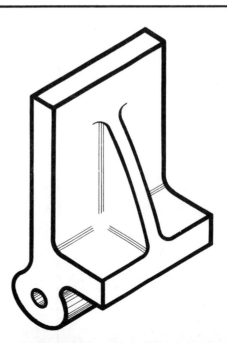

Draw freehand a pictorial view of the casting in isometric projection. Use an isometric grid, or drawing paper.

Make a freehand drawing of the wood chisel shown.

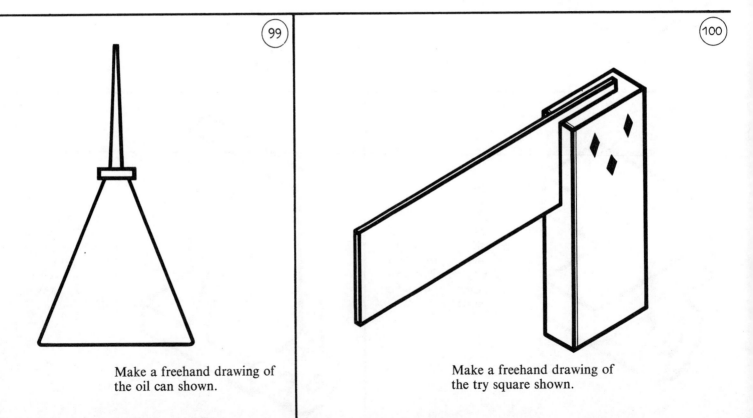

Make a freehand drawing of
the oil can shown.

Make a freehand drawing of
the try square shown.

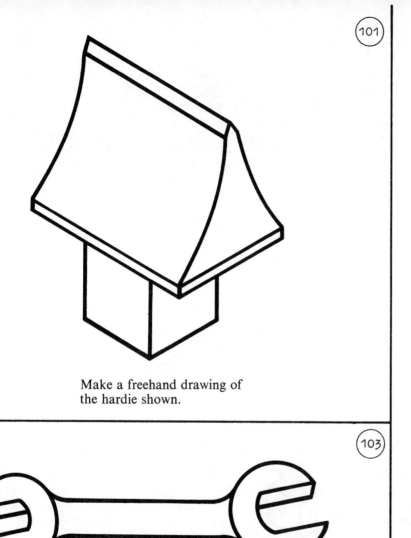

Make a freehand drawing of
the hardie shown.

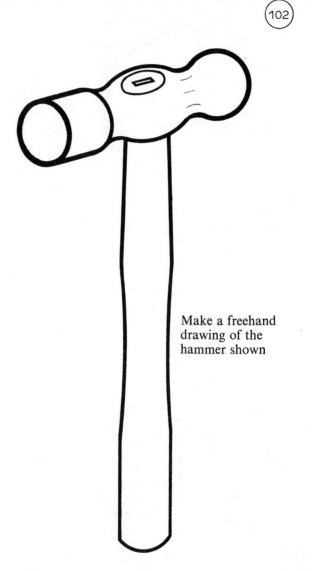

Make a freehand
drawing of the
hammer shown

Make a freehand drawing of
the spanner shown.

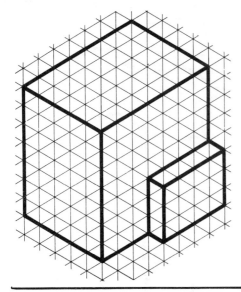

104

Draw the block in isometric projection on an isometric grid; or on drawing paper, assuming the isometric squares to be 10 millimetres.

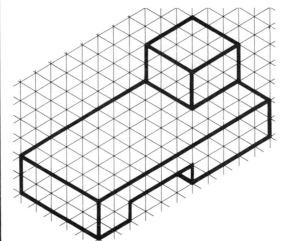

105

Draw the block in isometric projection on an isometric grid; or on drawing paper, assuming the isometric squares to be 10 millimetres.

106

Draw the block in isometric projection on an isometric grid; or on drawing paper, assuming the isometric squares to be 10 millimetres.

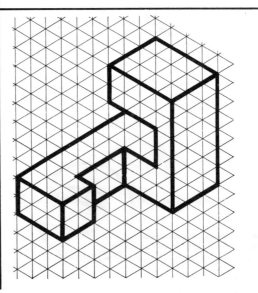

107

Draw the block in isometric projection on an isometric grid as shown or on drawing paper, assuming the isometric squares to be 10 millimetres.

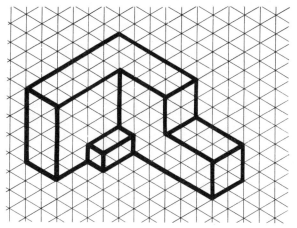

Draw the block in isometric projection as shown on an isometric grid; or on drawing paper, assuming the isometric squares to be 10 millimetres.

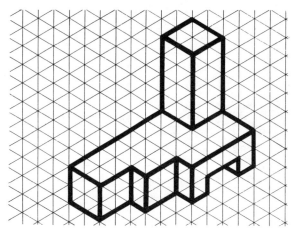

Draw the block in isometric projection as shown on an isometric grid; or on drawing paper, assuming the isometric squares to be 10 millimetres.

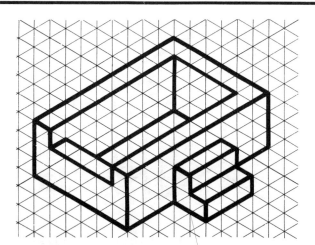

Draw the block in isometric projection as shown on an isometric grid; or on drawing paper, assuming the isometric squares to be 10 millimetres.

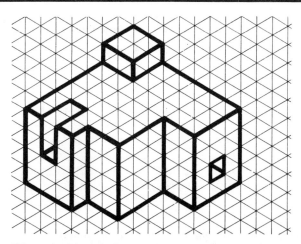

Draw the block in isometric projection as shown on an isometric grid; or on drawing paper, assuming the isometric squares to be 10 millimetres.

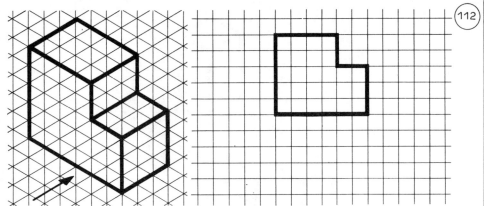

A front elevation of the block looking in the direction of the arrow has been drawn for you. From this project a plan and 2 end elevations. Use squared paper; or drawing paper, assuming the squares to be 10 millimetres.

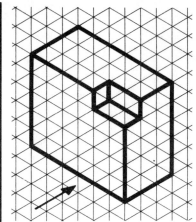

Draw:

1. A front elevation looking in the direction of the arrow.

2. A plan.

3. Two end elevations.

Use squared paper; or drawing paper, assuming the squares to be 10 millimetres.

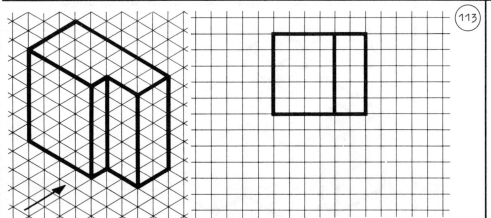

A front elevation of the block looking in the direction of the arrow has been drawn for you. From this project a plan and 2 end elevations. Use squared paper; or drawing paper, assuming the squares to be 10 millimetres.

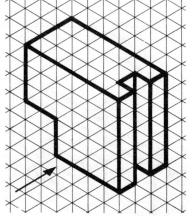

Draw:

1. A front elevation looking in the direction of the arrow.

2. A plan.

3. Two end elevations.

Use squared paper; or drawing paper, assuming the squares to be 10 millimetres.

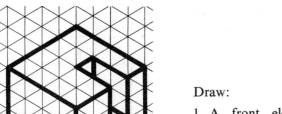

Draw:

1. A front elevation looking in the direction of the arrow.

2. A plan.

3. Two end elevations.

Use squared paper; or drawing paper, assuming the squares to be 10 millimetres.

Draw:

1. A front elevation looking in the direction of the arrow.

2. A plan.

3. Two end elevations.

Use squared paper; or drawing paper, assuming the squares to be 10 millimetres.

Draw:

1. A front elevation looking in the direction of the arrow.

2. A plan.

3. Two end elevations.

Use squared paper; or drawing paper, assuming the squares to be 10 millimetres.

Draw:

1. A front elevation looking in the direction of the arrow.

2. A plan.

3. Two end elevations.

Use squared paper; or drawing paper, assuming the squares to be 10 millimetres.

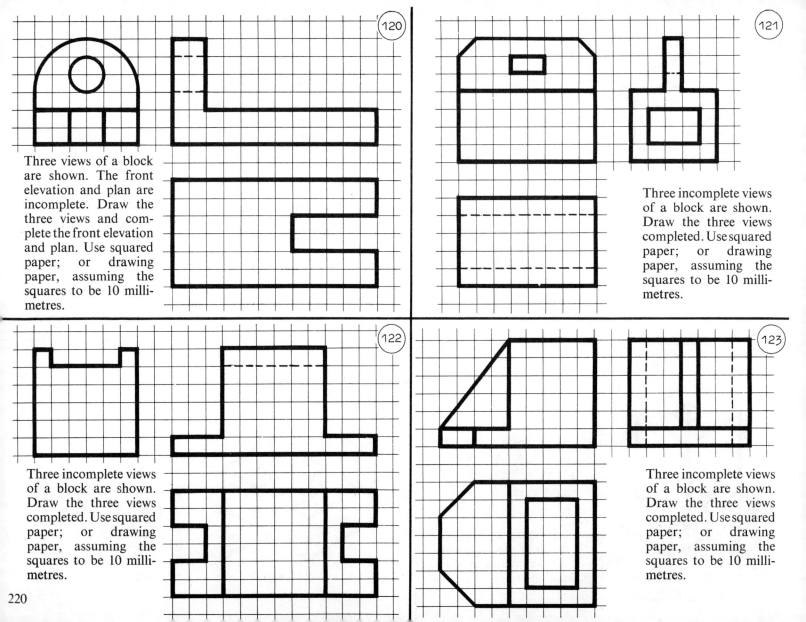

120

Three views of a block are shown. The front elevation and plan are incomplete. Draw the three views and complete the front elevation and plan. Use squared paper; or drawing paper, assuming the squares to be 10 millimetres.

121

Three incomplete views of a block are shown. Draw the three views completed. Use squared paper; or drawing paper, assuming the squares to be 10 millimetres.

122

Three incomplete views of a block are shown. Draw the three views completed. Use squared paper; or drawing paper, assuming the squares to be 10 millimetres.

123

Three incomplete views of a block are shown. Draw the three views completed. Use squared paper; or drawing paper, assuming the squares to be 10 millimetres.

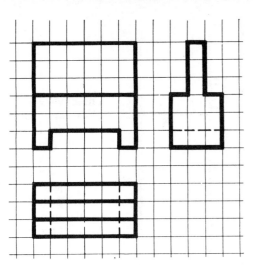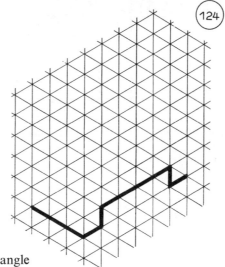

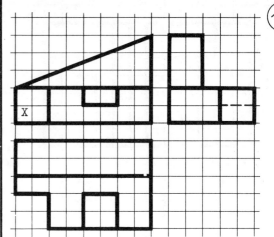

Three views of a block are shown in first angle projection and a start has been made on an isometric drawing of the block. Complete the isometric drawing. Use an isometric grid; or drawing paper, assuming the squares to be 10 millimetres.

Three views of a block are shown. Draw it in isometric projection on an isometric grid; or on drawing paper, assuming the squares to be 10 millimetres. Make X the lowest part of the drawing.

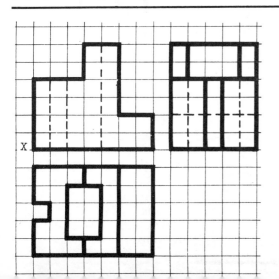

Three views of a block are shown. Draw it in isometric projection on an isometric grid; or on drawing paper, assuming the squares to be 10 millimetres. Make X the lowest part of the drawing.

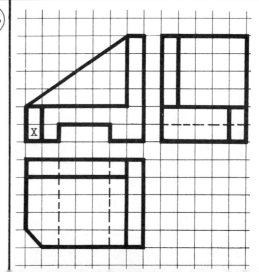

Three views of a block are shown. Draw it in isometric projection on an isometric grid; or on drawing paper, assuming the squares to be 10 millimetres. Make X the lowest part of the drawing.

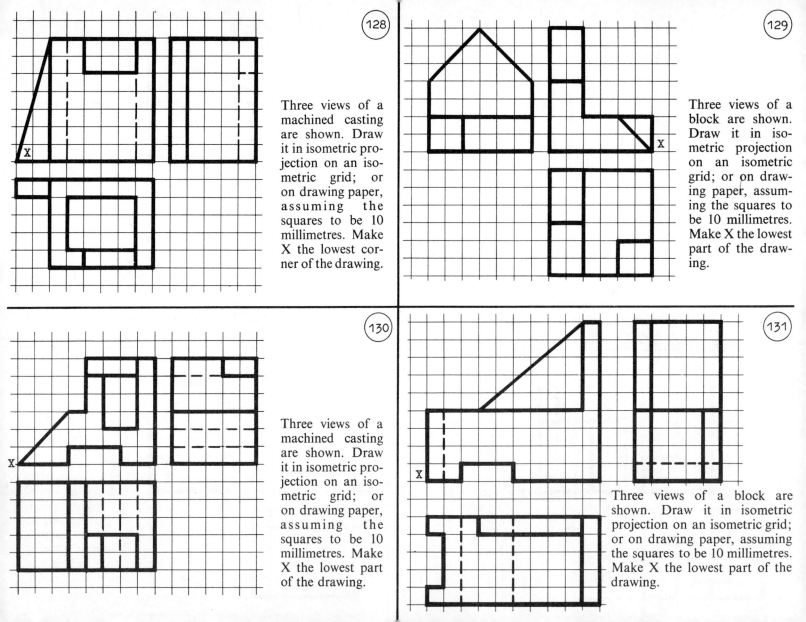

(128)

Three views of a machined casting are shown. Draw it in isometric projection on an isometric grid; or on drawing paper, assuming the squares to be 10 millimetres. Make X the lowest corner of the drawing.

(129)

Three views of a block are shown. Draw it in isometric projection on an isometric grid; or on drawing paper, assuming the squares to be 10 millimetres. Make X the lowest part of the drawing.

(130)

Three views of a machined casting are shown. Draw it in isometric projection on an isometric grid; or on drawing paper, assuming the squares to be 10 millimetres. Make X the lowest part of the drawing.

(131)

Three views of a block are shown. Draw it in isometric projection on an isometric grid; or on drawing paper, assuming the squares to be 10 millimetres. Make X the lowest part of the drawing.

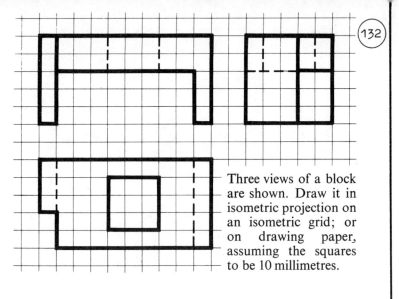

Three views of a block are shown. Draw it in isometric projection on an isometric grid; or on drawing paper, assuming the squares to be 10 millimetres.

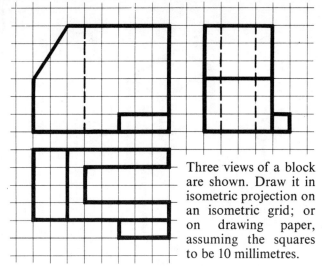

Three views of a block are shown. Draw it in isometric projection on an isometric grid; or on drawing paper, assuming the squares to be 10 millimetres.

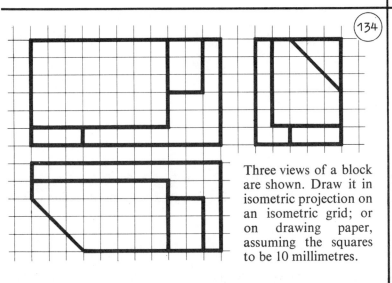

Three views of a block are shown. Draw it in isometric projection on an isometric grid; or on drawing paper, assuming the squares to be 10 millimetres.

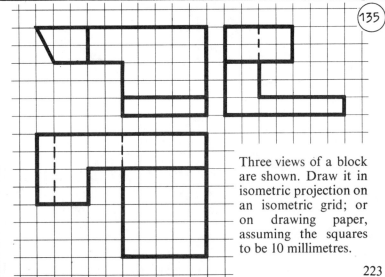

Three views of a block are shown. Draw it in isometric projection on an isometric grid; or on drawing paper, assuming the squares to be 10 millimetres.

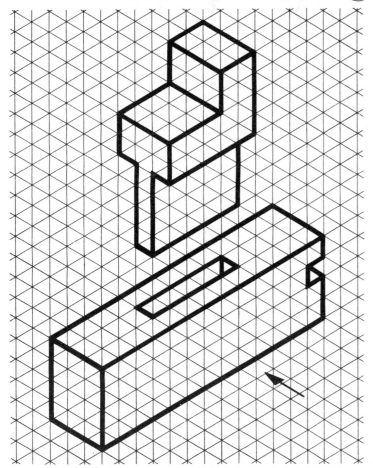

(136)

Assemble the two parts and draw:
1. A front elevation looking in the direction of the arrow.
2. A plan.
3. Two end elevations.
Use squared paper; or drawing paper, assuming the isometric squares to be 10 millimetres.

224

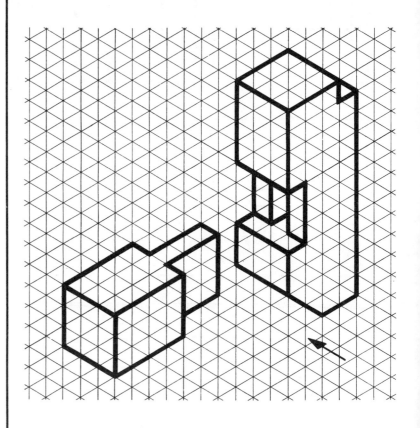

(137)

Assemble the two parts and draw:

1. A front elevation looking in the direction of the arrow.

2. A plan.

3. Two end elevations.

Use squared paper; or drawing paper, assuming the isometric squares to be 10 millimetres.

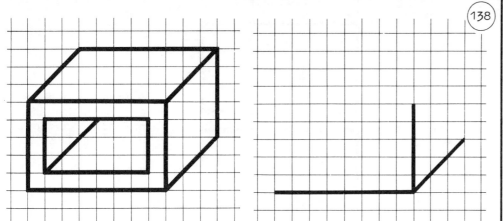

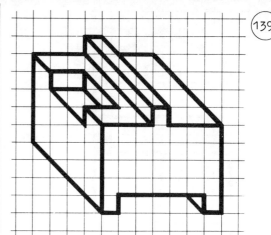

(138)

(139)

Draw the block in oblique projection as shown. A start has been made for you. Use squared paper; or drawing paper, assuming the squares to be 10 millimetres.

Draw the block in oblique projection as shown. Use squared paper; or drawing paper, assuming the squares to be 10 millimetres.

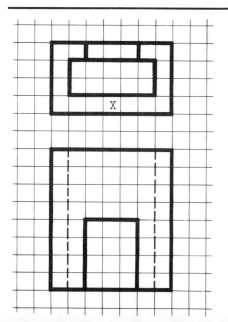

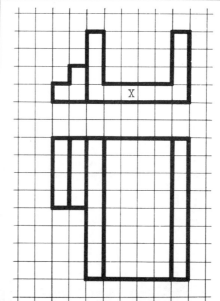

(140)

(141)

A front elevation and a plan, in first angle projection, are shown of a block. Draw the block in oblique projection, with face X parallel to the plane of projection. Use squared paper; or drawing paper, assuming the squares to be 10 millimetres.

A front elevation and a plan, in first angle projection, are shown of a block. Draw the block in oblique projection, with face X parallel to the plane of projection. Use squared paper; or drawing paper, assuming the squares to be 10 millimetres.

225

(142)

A front elevation and a plan, in first angle projection, are shown of a block. Draw the block in oblique projection, with face X parallel to the plane of projection. Use squared paper; or drawing paper, assuming the squares to be 10 millimetres.

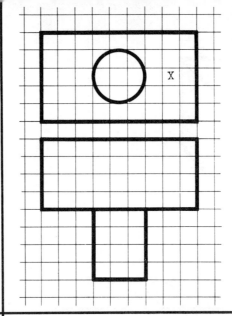

(143)

A front elevation and a plan, in first angle projection, are shown of a block. Draw the block in oblique projection, with face X parallel to the plane of projection. Use squared paper; or drawing paper, assuming the squares to be 10 millimetres.

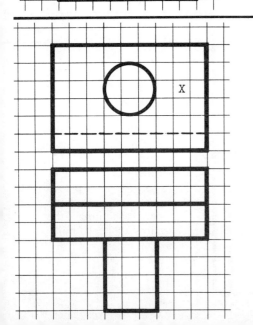

(144)

A front elevation and a plan, in first angle projection, are shown of a block. Draw the block in oblique projection, with face X parallel to the plane of projection. Use squared paper; or drawing paper, assuming the squares to be 10 millimetres.

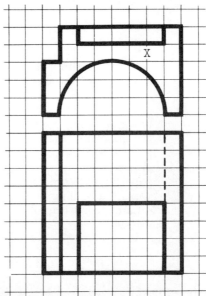

(145)

A front elevation and a plan, in first angle projection, are shown of a block. Draw the block in oblique projection, with face X parallel to the plane of projection. Use squared paper; or drawing paper, assuming the squares to be 10 millimetres.

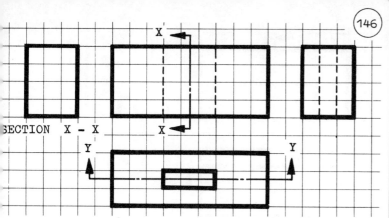

SECTION X - X

A front elevation, a plan, an end elevation, and an incomplete section X–X, are shown of a block. Draw these views and complete the section X–X. Also draw a section on plane Y–Y. Use squared paper; or drawing paper, assuming the squares to be 10 millimetres.

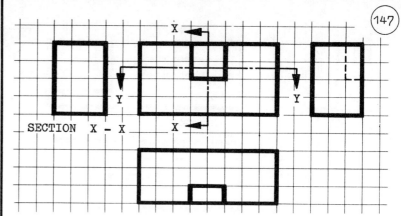

SECTION X - X

A front elevation, a plan, an end elevation, and an incomplete section X–X, are shown of a block. Draw these views and complete the section X–X. Also draw a section on plane Y–Y. Use squared paper; or drawing paper, assuming the squares to be 10 millimetres.

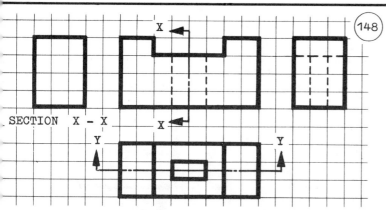

SECTION X - X

A front elevation, a plan, an end elevation, and an incomplete section X–X, are shown of a block. Draw these views and complete the section X–X. Also draw a section on plane Y–Y. Use squared paper; or drawing paper, assuming the squares to be 10 millimetres.

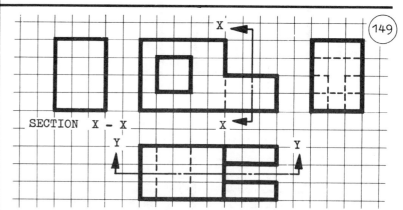

SECTION X - X

A front elevation, a plan, an end elevation, and an incomplete section X–X, are shown of a block. Draw these views and complete the section X–X. Also draw a section on plane Y–Y. Use squared paper; or drawing paper, assuming the squares to be 10 millimetres.

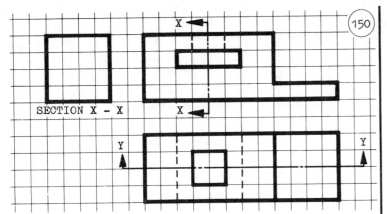

(150)

SECTION X - X

A front elevation, a plan, and an incomplete section X–X, are shown of a block. Draw these views and complete the section X–X. Also draw a section on plane Y–Y. Use squared paper; or drawing paper, assuming the squares to be 10 millimetres.

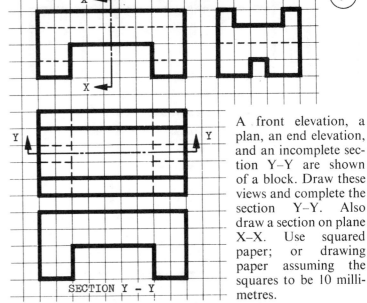

(151)

SECTION Y - Y

A front elevation, a plan, an end elevation, and an incomplete section Y–Y are shown of a block. Draw these views and complete the section Y–Y. Also draw a section on plane X–X. Use squared paper; or drawing paper assuming the squares to be 10 millimetres.

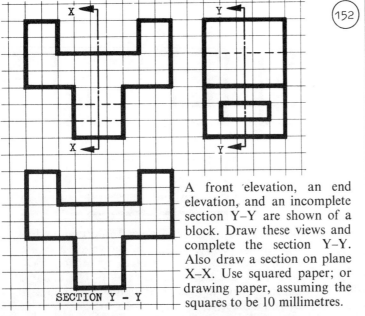

(152)

SECTION Y - Y

A front elevation, an end elevation, and an incomplete section Y–Y are shown of a block. Draw these views and complete the section Y–Y. Also draw a section on plane X–X. Use squared paper; or drawing paper, assuming the squares to be 10 millimetres.

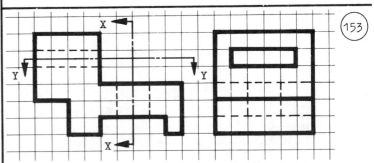

(153)

A front elevation and an end elevation of a block are shown. Draw these views, and the sections X–X and Y–Y. Use squared paper; or drawing paper, assuming the squares to be 10 millimetres.

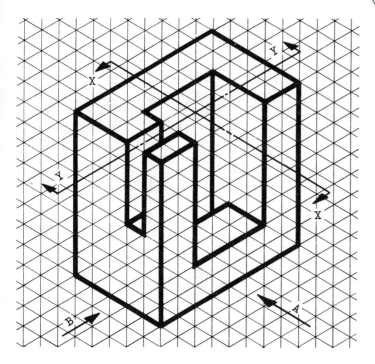

Draw: ·

1. A front elevation looking in the direction of arrow A.

2. A plan.

3. An end elevation looking in the direction of arrow B.

4. A section on plane X–X.

5. A section on plane Y–Y.

Use squared paper; or drawing paper, assuming the squares to be 10 millimetres.

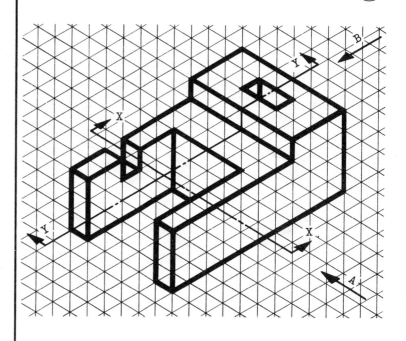

Draw:

1. A front elevation looking in the direction of arrow A.

2. A plan.

3. An end elevation looking in the direction of arrow B.

4. A section on plane X–X.

5. A section on plane Y–Y.

Use squared paper; or drawing paper, assuming the squares to be 10 millimetres.

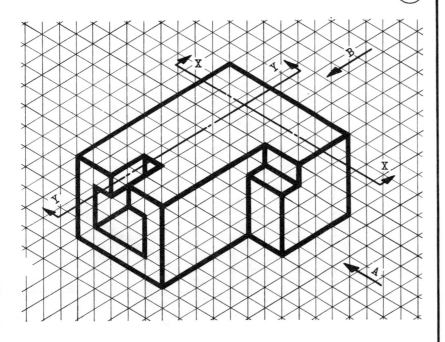

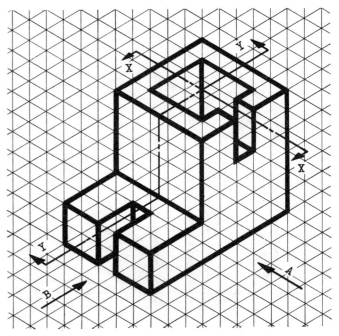

Draw:

1. A front elevation looking in the direction of arrow A.

2. A plan.

3. An end elevation looking in the direction of arrow B.

4. A section on plane X–X.

5. A section on plane Y–Y.

Use squared paper; or drawing paper, assuming the squares to be 10 millimetres.

Draw:

1. A front elevation looking in the direction of arrow A.

2. A plan.

3. An end elevation looking in the direction of arrow B.

4. A section on plane X–X.

5. A section on plane Y–Y.

Use squared paper; or drawing paper, assuming the squares to be 10 millimetres.

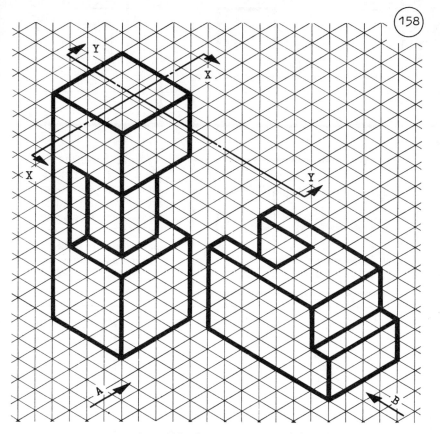

Assemble the two parts and draw:
1. A front elevation looking in the direction of arrow A.
2. A plan.
3. An end elevation looking in the direction of arrow B.
4. A section on plane X–X.
5. A section on plane Y–Y.
Use squared paper; or drawing paper, assuming the squares to be 10 millimetres.

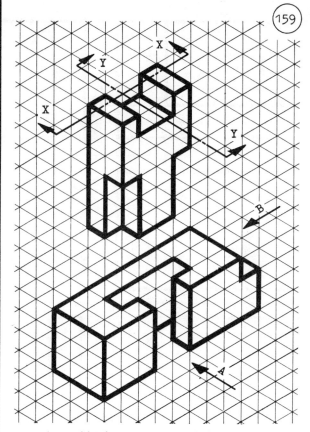

Assemble the two parts and draw:
1. A front elevation looking in the direction on arrow A.
2. A plan.
3. An end elevation looking in the direction of arrow B.
4. A section on plane X–X.
5. A section on plane Y–Y.
Use squared paper; or drawing paper, assuming the squares to be 10 millimetres.

231

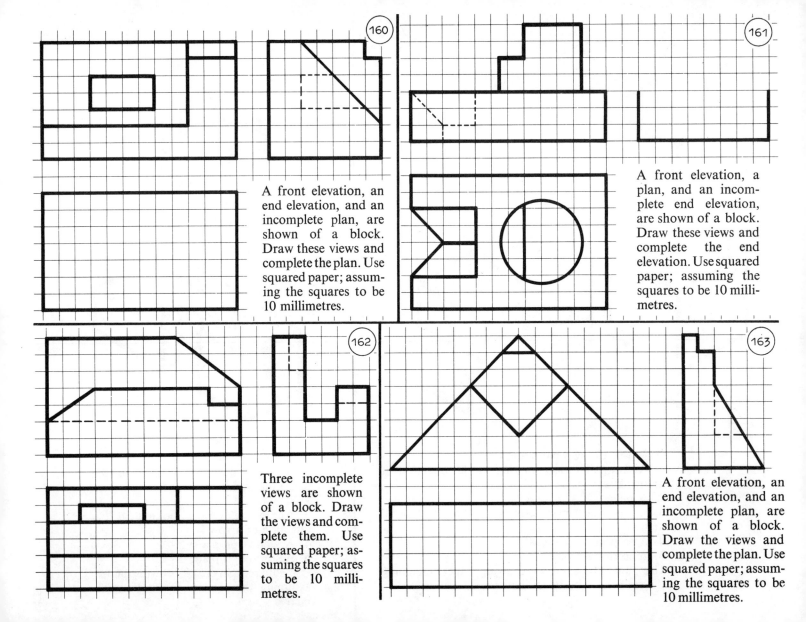

160

A front elevation, an end elevation, and an incomplete plan, are shown of a block. Draw these views and complete the plan. Use squared paper; assuming the squares to be 10 millimetres.

161

A front elevation, a plan, and an incomplete end elevation, are shown of a block. Draw these views and complete the end elevation. Use squared paper; assuming the squares to be 10 millimetres.

162

Three incomplete views are shown of a block. Draw the views and complete them. Use squared paper; assuming the squares to be 10 millimetres.

163

A front elevation, an end elevation, and an incomplete plan, are shown of a block. Draw the views and complete the plan. Use squared paper; assuming the squares to be 10 millimetres.

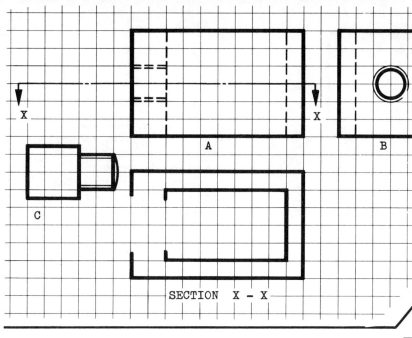

SECTION X - X

First Angle Projection

Draw C (shaft) assembled in A and B (casting). Then complete the section X–X. Use squared paper; or drawing paper, assuming the squares to be 10 millimetres.

(164)

First Angle Projection

Draw C (shaft) and D (ring-nut) assembled on A and B (bracket). Then draw a section on plane X–X. Use squared paper; or drawing paper, assuming the squares to be 10 millimetres.

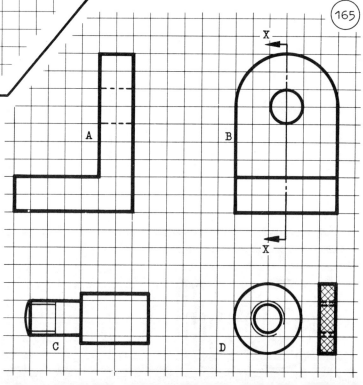

(165)

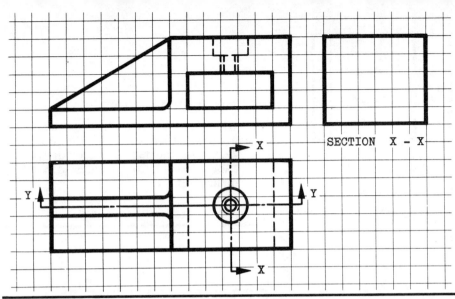

SECTION X - X

First Angle Projection

Draw a front elevation and plan of the casting as shown, and complete the section X–X. Also draw a section on plane Y–Y. Use squared paper; or drawing paper, assuming the squares to be 10 millimetres.

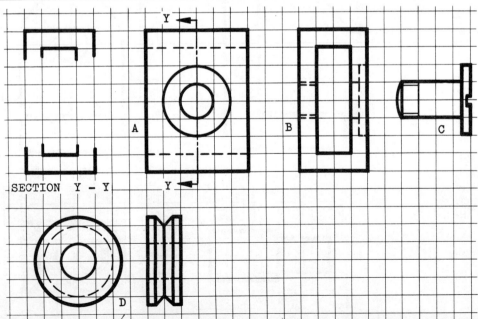

SECTION Y - Y

First Angle Projection

Draw D and C assembled in A and B. Then complete the section Y–Y. Use squared paper; or drawing paper, assuming the squares to be 10 millimetres.

Third Angle Projection

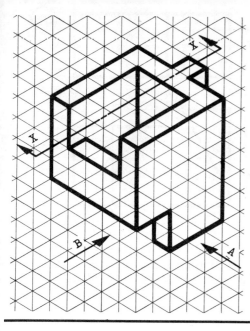

Draw:

1. A front elevation looking in the direction of arrow A.

2. A plan.

3. An end elevation looking in the direction of arrow B.

4. A section on plane X–X.

Use squared paper; or drawing paper, assuming the squares to be 10 millimetres.

Third Angle Projection

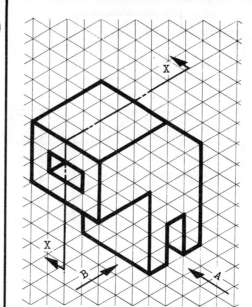

Draw:

1. A front elevation looking in the direction of arrow A.

2. A plan.

3. An end elevation looking in the direction of arrow B.

4. A section on plane X–X.

Use squared paper; or drawing paper, assuming the squares to be 10 millimetres.

Third Angle Projection

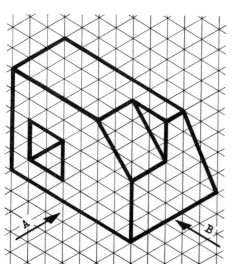

Draw:

1. A front elevation looking in the direction of arrow A.

2. An end elevation looking in the direction of arrow B.

3. A plan.

Use squared paper; or drawing paper, assuming the squares to be 10 millimetres.

Third Angle Projection

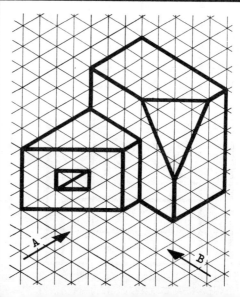

Draw:

1. A front elevation looking in the direction of arrow A.

2. A plan.

3. An end elevation looking in the direction of arrow B.

Use squared paper; or drawing paper, assuming the squares to be 10 millimetres.

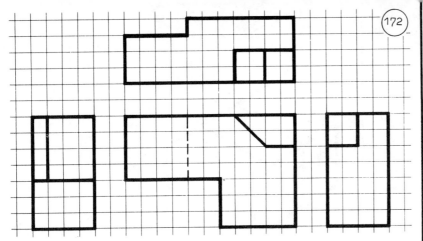

Third Angle Projection

Four incomplete views of a block are shown. Draw and complete them. Use squared paper; assuming the squares to be 10 millimetres.

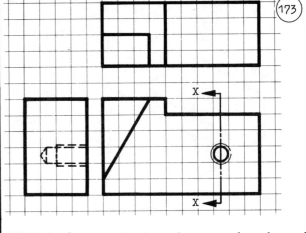

Third Angle Projection

Draw the three views, complete plan and end elevation, and draw a section on plane X–X. Use squared paper; assuming the squares to be 10 millimetres.

Third Angle Projection

Draw views, and complete section X–X. Use squared paper, assuming the squares to be 10 millimetres.

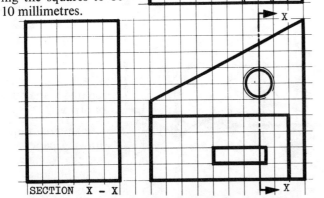

SECTION X – X

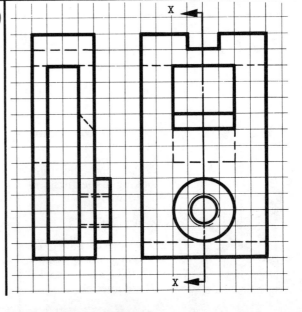

Third Angle Projection

Draw the two views, and project a plan and a section on plane X–X. Use squared paper; or drawing paper, assuming the squares to be 10 millimetres.

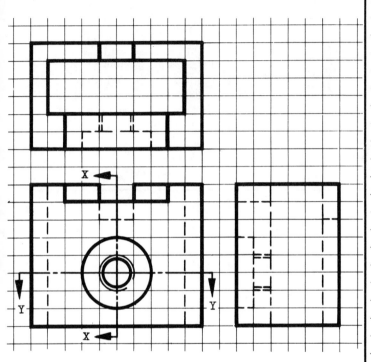

Third Angle Projection

Three views of a machined casting are shown. Draw these views, and also the sections X–X and Y–Y. Use squared paper; or drawing paper, assuming the squares to be 10 millimetres.

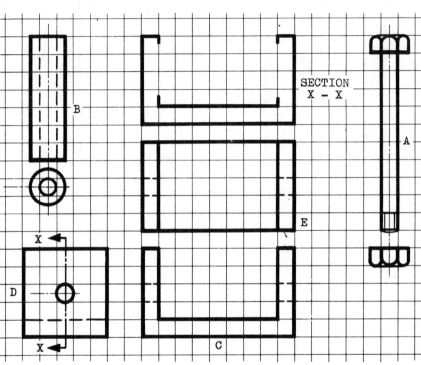

Third Angle Projection

Draw B (roller) and A (nut and bolt) assembled in C, D, E. Then complete the section X–X. Use squared paper; or drawing paper, assuming the squares to be 10 millimetres.

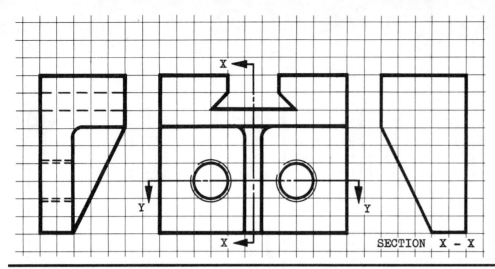

Third Angle Projection

Draw the front elevation and the end elevation of the casting as shown. Complete the section X–X, and draw a section on plane Y–Y. Use squared paper; or drawing paper, assuming the squares to be 10 millimetres.

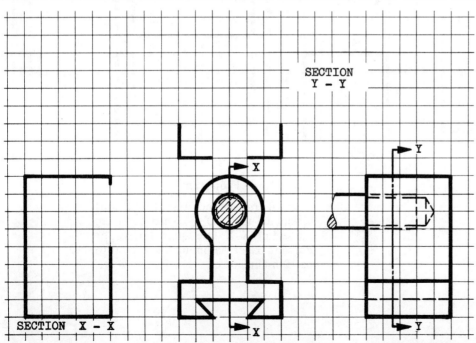

Third Angle Projection

Draw the front elevation and the end elevation as shown, and complete the two sections X–X and Y–Y. Use squared paper; or drawing paper, assuming the squares to be 10 millimetres.

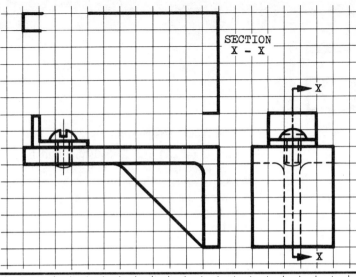

SECTION
X – X

Third Angle Projection

Draw the front elevation and the end elevation as shown. Project a plan, and complete the section X–X. Use squared paper; or drawing paper assuming the squares to be 10 millimetres.

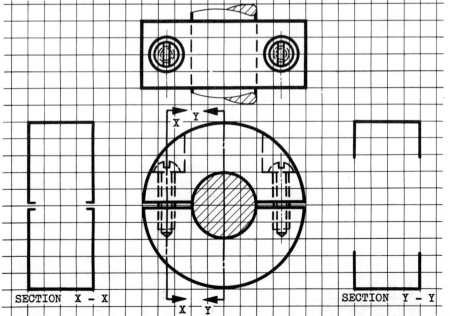

SECTION   X – X

SECTION   Y – Y

Third Angle Projection

Draw the front elevation and the plan as shown, and complete the two sections X–X and Y–Y. Use squared paper; or drawing paper, assuming the squares to be 10 millimetres.

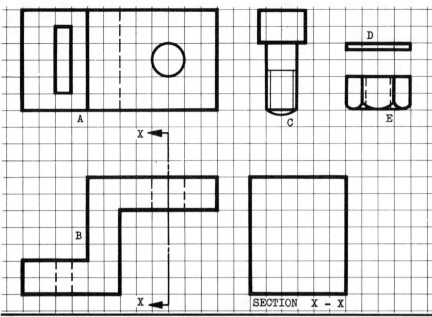

Third Angle Projection

Draw C (shaft) and D (washer) and E (nut) assembled in A and B (bracket). Then complete the section X–X. Use squared paper; or drawing paper, assuming the squares to be 10 millimetres.

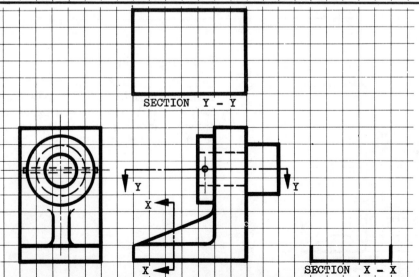

Third Angle Projection

Draw the front elevation and the end elevation as shown, and complete the two sections X–X and Y–Y. Use squared paper; or drawing paper, assuming the squares to be 10 millimetres.

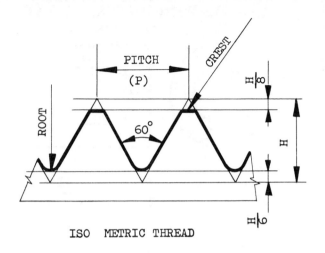

ISO METRIC THREAD

SCREW THREADS

The ISO Metric thread is designated by the letter M, followed by the nominal diameter and the pitch in millimetres. e.g. M6×0·75. If the pitch is not stated, it is a coarse thread, e.g. M6.

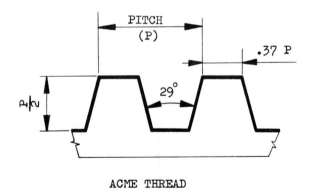

ACME THREAD

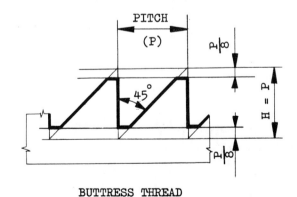

BUTTRESS THREAD

The Acme and Buttress threads are used to transmit power.

CONVENTIONAL METHODS OF DRAWING EXTERNAL VEE THREADS

CONVENTIONAL METHODS OF DRAWING INTERNAL VEE THREADS

242   The edge of a screw thread is really a helix, but since this takes time to draw, speedy conventional methods are used instead.

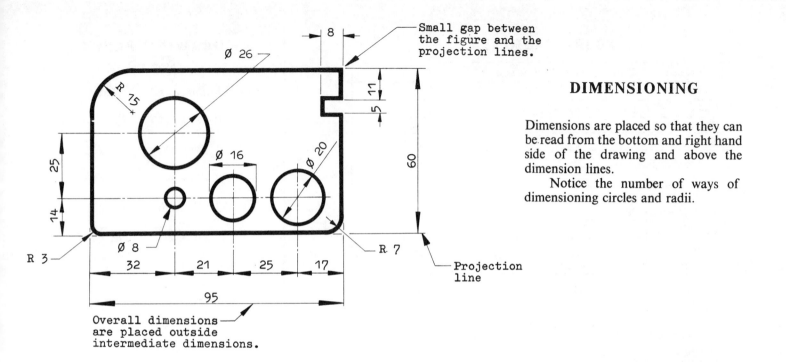

Ø 26

R 15

Small gap between
the figure and the
projection lines.

8

11

5

60

Ø 16

Ø 20

25

14

R 3

Ø 8

32   21   25   17

R 7

Projection
line

95

Overall dimensions
are placed outside
intermediate dimensions.

DIMENSIONING

Dimensions are placed so that they can be read from the bottom and right hand side of the drawing and above the dimension lines.

Notice the number of ways of dimensioning circles and radii.

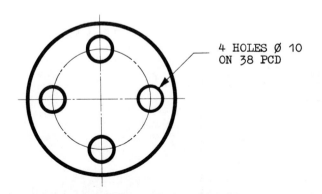

4 HOLES Ø 10
ON 38 PCD

Holes are often defined so that they are equidistant from each other on a pitch circle of given diameter (P C D).

ABBREVIATIONS

Diameter (before the dimension)	Ø
Diameter (in a note)	DIA
Radius (before the dimension)	R
Chamfered	CHAM
Millimetre	mm
Centimetre	cm
Metre ·	m
Countersunk	CSK
Countersunk head	CSK HD
Centre line	₵
Number	NO.
Square (before the dimension)	□
Square (in a note)	SQ
Outside diameter	O/D
Inside diameter	I/D
Threads per inch	TPI
Hexagon	HEX
Hexagonal head	HEX HD
Across flats	A/F
Round head	RD HD
Right hand	RH
Left hand	LH
Pitch circle diameter	PCD
Counterbore	C'BORE
Figure	FIG.
Drawing	DRG
Material	MATL
Centres	CRS

Full stops are not used unless the abbreviation makes a word, e.g. FIG.

DRAWING PAPER SIZES

	Millimetres	Inches
A0	841×1189	$33\frac{1}{8} \times 46\frac{3}{4}$
A1	594×841	$23\frac{3}{8} \times 33\frac{1}{8}$
A2	420×594	$16\frac{1}{2} \times 23\frac{3}{8}$
A3	297×420	$11\frac{3}{4} \times 16\frac{1}{2}$
A4	210×297	$8\frac{1}{4} \times 11\frac{3}{4}$

A copy of *Engineering Drawing Practice*, B.S. 308, can be obtained from the British Standards Institution, 2 Park Street, London, W.1.

HEXAGONAL-HEADED NUT AND BOLT

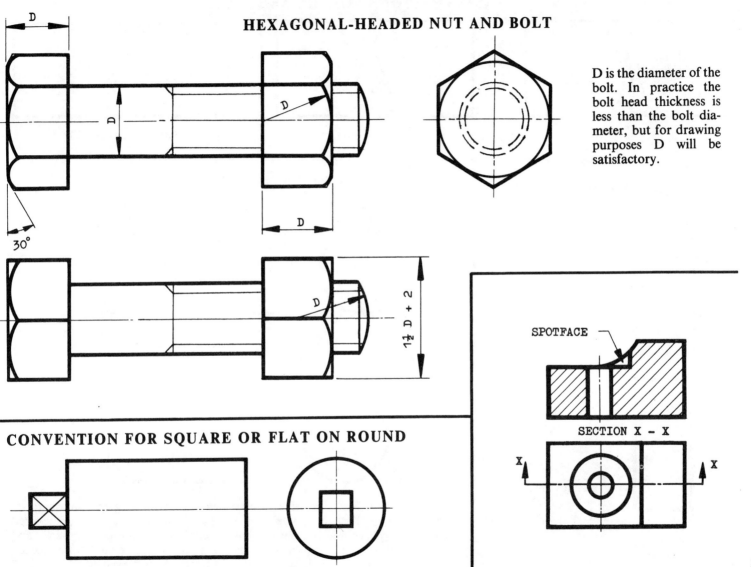

D is the diameter of the bolt. In practice the bolt head thickness is less than the bolt diameter, but for drawing purposes D will be satisfactory.

$1\frac{1}{2}D + 2$

CONVENTION FOR SQUARE OR FLAT ON ROUND

SPOTFACE

SECTION X - X

CONVENTIONS FOR BREAKS

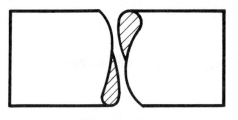

ROUND – SOLID

ROUND – TUBE

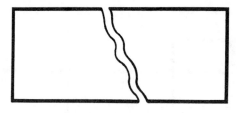

SQUARE OR RECTANGULAR

CONVENTIONS FOR KNURLING

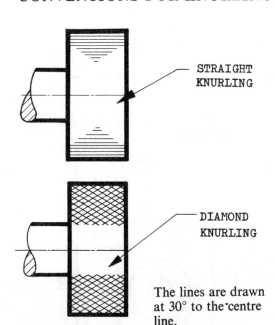

STRAIGHT KNURLING

DIAMOND KNURLING

The lines are drawn at 30° to the centre line.

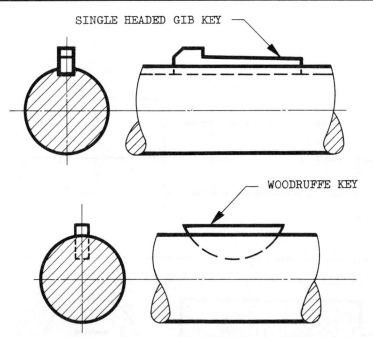

SINGLE HEADED GIB KEY

WOODRUFFE KEY

A key is used to stop a piece of machinery from rotating in relation to its adjoining part. Keys may be placed into two groups: those which are tapered and are driven in and prevent any movement between the mating parts, and those which are untapered (feather keys) and often designed so that the mating pieces may slide freely along the shaft, but rotation is prevented.

SET SCREWS AND BOLTS

ROUND
HEAD

COUNTERSUNK
HEAD

HEXAGONAL
HEAD

CHEESE
HEAD

PHILLIPS
HEAD

ALLEN
HEAD

A set screw is similar to a bolt except that it is threaded the whole length or stopped at a distance not exceeding twice the pitch of the thread from the underside of the head.

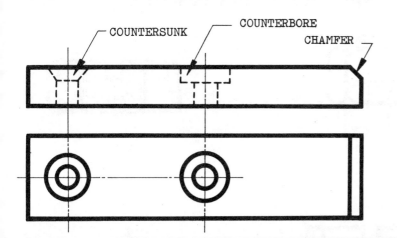

COUNTERSUNK

COUNTERBORE

CHAMFER

THUMB SCREW

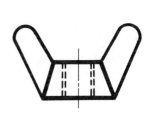

WING NUT

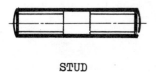

STUD

GRUB SCREW

WASHER

RIVETS

| FLAT HEAD | PAN HEAD | COUNTERSUNK HEAD | SNAP HEAD |

These are mainly used for locking nuts.

SPLIT PIN   SOLID TAPER PIN

SET SCREW POINTS

CHAMFERED   ROUND

CONICAL   DOG

NUT LOCKING DEVICES

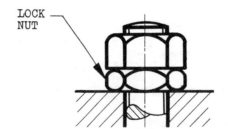

LOCK NUT

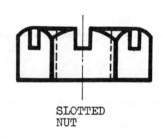

SLOTTED NUT

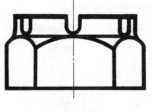

CASTLE NUT

There is always a danger of nuts unscrewing due to vibration, and for this reason they are often locked in position.

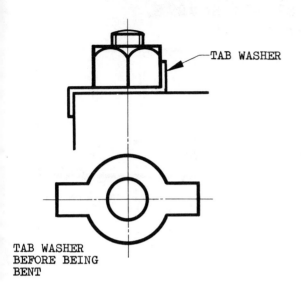

TAB WASHER

TAB WASHER
BEFORE BEING
BENT

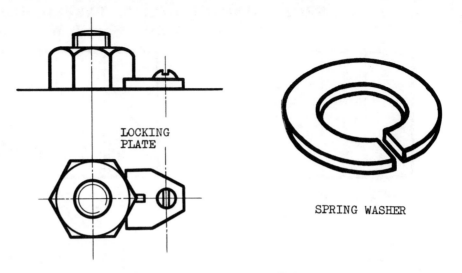

LOCKING
PLATE

SPRING WASHER

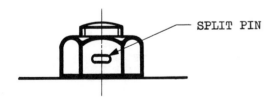

SPLIT PIN

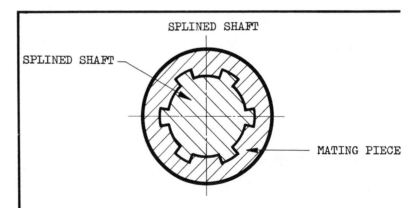

SPLINED SHAFT

SPLINED SHAFT

MATING PIECE

When a shaft is to carry a heavy load a
splined shaft is used instead of a feather
key. Splined shafts are widely used in
aeroplane and motor-car engineering.

SECTIONING OF HOLES, TAPPED HOLES, SET SCREWS, NUTS AND BOLTS AND WASHERS, RIVETS

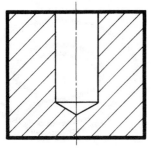

SECTION THROUGH A
DRILLED HOLE

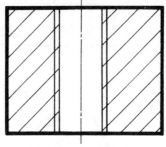

SECTION THROUGH A
TAPPED HOLE

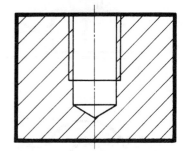

SECTION THROUGH A DRILLED
AND TAPPED HOLE

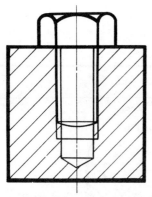

SECTION THROUGH A DRILLED AND
TAPPED HOLE WITH A SET SCREW

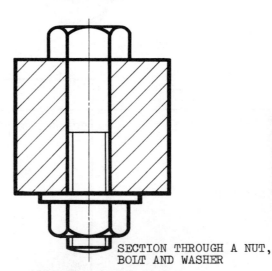

SECTION THROUGH A NUT,
BOLT AND WASHER

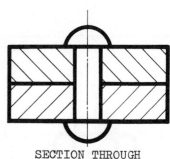

SECTION THROUGH
A RIVET

Although we cut through the centre of a set screw in a section, we do not section it. It is shown as an outside view.

Although we cut through the centre of a nut, bolt and washer in a section, we do not section them. They are shown as an outside view.

Although we cut through the centre of a rivet in a section, we do not section it. It is shown as an outside view.

BEARINGS

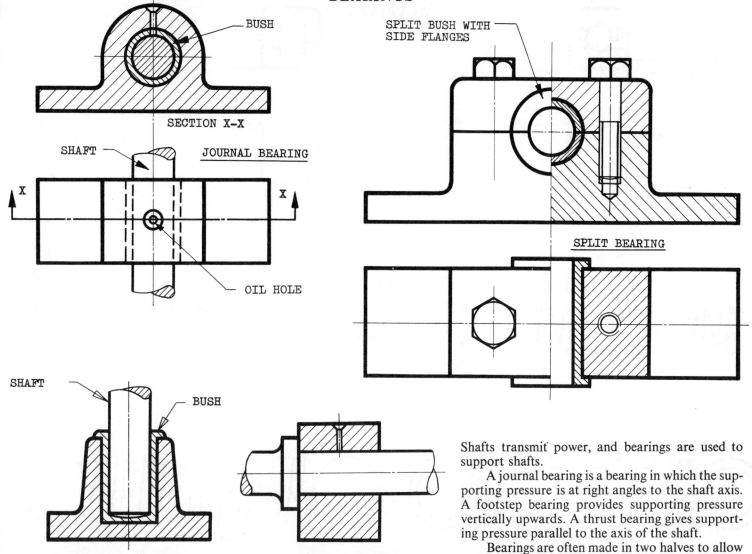

BUSH

SECTION X-X

SHAFT

JOURNAL BEARING

OIL HOLE

SPLIT BUSH WITH
SIDE FLANGES

SPLIT BEARING

SHAFT

BUSH

FOOTSTEP BEARING

THRUST BEARING

Shafts transmit power, and bearings are used to support shafts.

A journal bearing is a bearing in which the supporting pressure is at right angles to the shaft axis. A footstep bearing provides supporting pressure vertically upwards. A thrust bearing gives supporting pressure parallel to the axis of the shaft.

Bearings are often made in two halves to allow for easy assembly.

251

BEARINGS

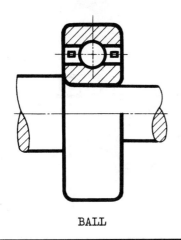

BALL

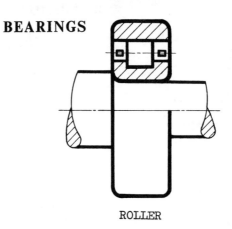

ROLLER

SPRINGS

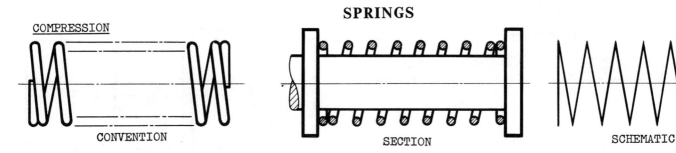

COMPRESSION

CONVENTION

SECTION

SCHEMATIC

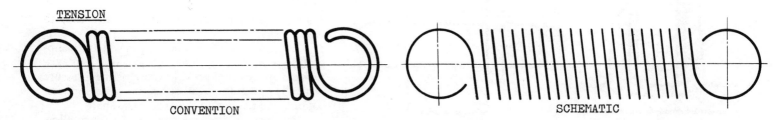

TENSION

CONVENTION

SCHEMATIC

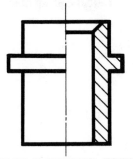

HALF SECTIONAL VIEW

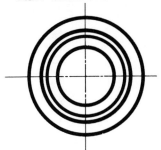

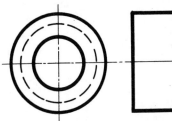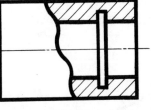

PART SECTIONAL VIEW

Part sectional views are helpful for showing important detail.

Many components are symmetrical about a centre line and it is often useful to produce a view in which one half is in full elevation and the other half is in section.

LUG

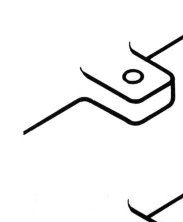

1

2

BOSS

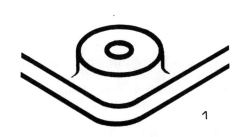

1

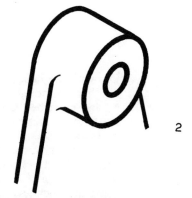

2

253

To Construct the Front View of a Helical Spring made from Circular Rod

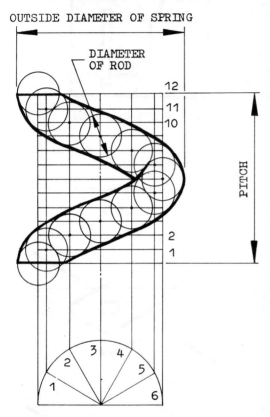

OUTSIDE DIAMETER OF SPRING

DIAMETER OF ROD

PITCH

To Construct the Front View of a Helical Spring made from Square Section Material

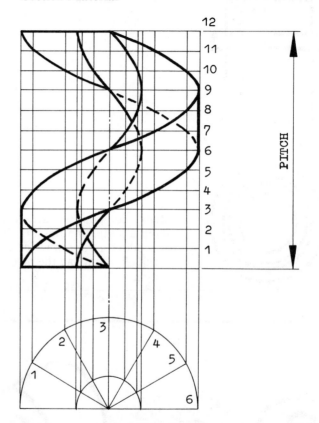

PITCH

Mark the points for the helix formed by the centre line of the spring. It is not necessary to actually draw the centre line helix. At the points found for the centre line, draw circles the same diameter as the rod. Draw freehand curves tangential to the circles, and complete by continuing the upper half of the helix on to the centre line at the turn.

Drawing the helical spring involves drawing two helices, one within another. Although the diameters of the helices are different, their pitches must be the same. When the points have been plotted, it is a matter of sorting out which parts of the helices can be seen and which parts are hidden.

For clarity, the thickness of the material is $\frac{1}{4}$ of the pitch of the helix. If the thickness is not a convenient fraction, it is necessary to set out the pitch twice. The measurement between the two pitches being the thickness of the material.

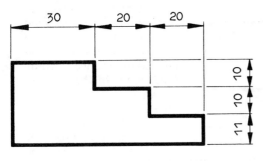

CHAIN DIMENSIONING

This is the commonest form of dimensioning. The advantages of this method are that the size of each feature is easy to read and it is economical with space. The disadvantage is due to the fact that errors in measurement can be cumulative, totaling up to a large error on the overall size.

DATUM DIMENSIONING

The great advantage of this method is that each size is measured independently from one edge, and consequently errors are not cumulative.

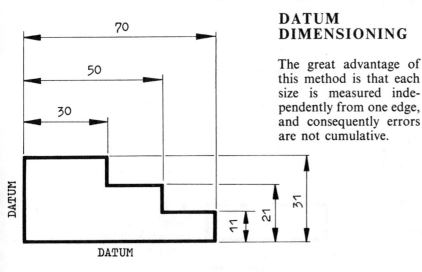

CONVENTIONAL REPRESENTATION OF MATERIALS

GLASS

WOOD

INSULATION

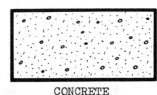

CONCRETE

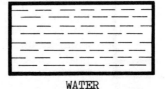

WATER

With the exception of the above, ordinary section lining should be used in all cases where materials are shown in section.

When it is an advantage to indicate materials by colours, the following are used: steel—purple; brass, phosphor bronze and gunmetal—light yellow; aluminium and tin—light green; glass—pale blue wash; brickwork—vermilion; earth—sepia.

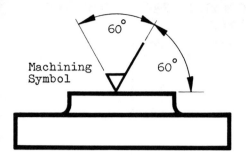

Machining Symbol

MACHINING SYMBOLS

Engineering components may be forged, cast, etc., and it is often necessary to machine some of the faces. It is important that these machined faces are indicated on the drawing.

The small tick only indicates that the particular face has to be machined. It does not state how smooth the finish is to be.

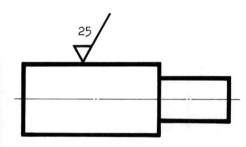

When the surface of machined metal is magnified it has the appearance of a range of mountains. The surface roughness is the distance from the highest peak to the lowest valley. This roughness is measured in micrometres. (A micrometre is a millionth part of a metre.) Refer to British Standards for index numbers.

The surface roughness number is placed above the symbol as shown.

If a special process such as lapping, honing, scraping, etc., is required to produce a surface finish, the appropriate process should be specified.

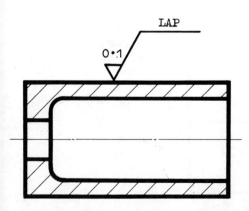

TOLERANCES

Tolerances make it possible for mass-produced parts to be interchangeable. A tolerance is a permitted range of error.

Tolerances may be calculated to produce a certain kind of fit. In the example shown the shaft is a clearance fit in the hole.

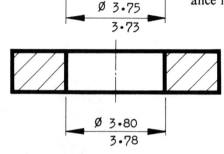

The larger limit of size should be given first. In this method both limits of size are specified.

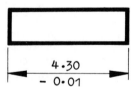

Another method is to specify one limit of size with a limit of tolerance in one direction.

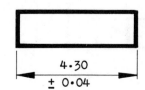

A further method is to specify a size with limits of tolerance above and below the size.

ELECTRONICS SYMBOLS

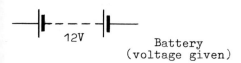

Battery
(voltage given)

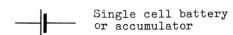

Single cell battery
or accumulator

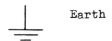

Earth

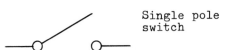

Single pole
switch

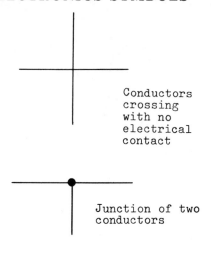

Conductors
crossing
with no
electrical
contact

Junction of two
conductors

Socket

Plug

Direct Current
(D.C.)

Alternating
Current (A.C)

Fuse

Fixed resistor

Variable resistor

Loudspeaker

LED

(Light emitting diode)

257

ELECTRONICS SYMBOLS

—||— Capacitor

Winding of an inductor, coil etc.

 Electric bell

Amplifier

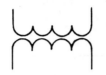 Transformer

(A) Ammeter

(V) Voltmeter

(M) Motor

(G) Generator

 Filament lamp

 Signal lamp

+ Positive polarity

— Negative polarity

O Terminal or tag

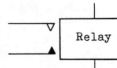 Relay

ELECTRICAL CIRCUITS

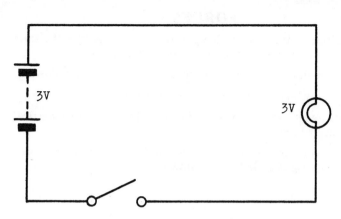

Simple circuit of battery, lamp and switch. The 3-volt battery will light the 3-volt bulb when the switch is made.

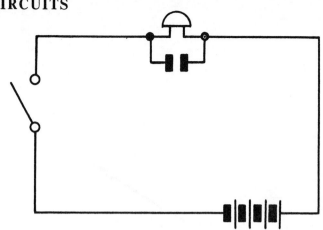

Four-cell battery connected to bell via switch. When the switch is made, the bell will ring. The capacitor causes sharper current impulses across the bell winding.

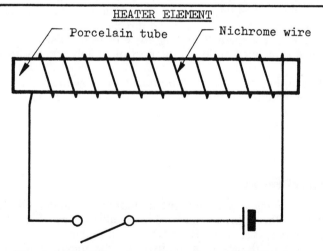

HEATER ELEMENT

The heater element consists of a nickel-chrome resistance wire wrapped round a porcelain tube.

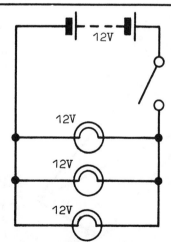

Simple parallel circuit. The 12-volt battery will light three 12-volt bulbs when the switch is made.

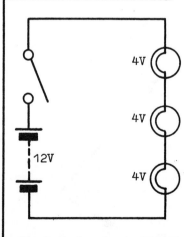

Simple series circuit. The 12-volt battery will light three 4-volt bulbs when the switch is made.

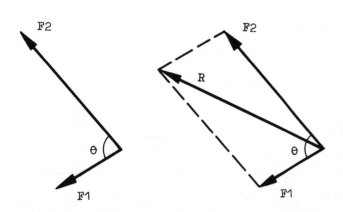

FORCES

Force is defined as that which changes, or tends to change, the state of rest of a body or its uniform motion in a straight line.

In order to describe a force it is necessary to know the following:

1. Magnitude—which means the size of the force.

2. Direction—which means the line of action of the force (e.g. vertical horizontal, or otherwise).

3. Sense—this means which way along the line of action the force is acting (e.g. right or left, up or down).

Graphical Representation of Force

The above mentioned characteristics of a force can be represented graphically by using a line called a vector. A vector is a straight line of definite length and direction, with an arrowhead to indicate sense, and represents to scale the magnitude and direction.

We will consider a force P pulling away from a point O on a body. The force is inclined at 30° to the horizontal and acts towards the right.

The line OP is drawn to a scale to represent the magnitude of the force P, and the direction of the force is represented by the line being drawn at 30° to the horizontal. The arrowhead shows the sense as pulling away from O.

Parallelogram of Forces

When two forces acting at a given point are represented in magnitude and direction by the adjacent sides of a parallelogram, then the resultant (a resultant is a single force which will replace an existing system of forces) of these forces is given by the diagonal of the parallelogram.

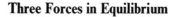

Space diagram

Three Forces in Equilibrium

If three forces in the same plane (coplanar forces) are in equilibrium and the lines of action pass through a common point, they can be represented in magnitude and direction by the sides of a triangle drawn to scale. This is called the 'triangle of forces'.

The three coplanar forces are shown acting on a body which is in equilibrium. The point O, where the lines of action of the forces meet, is called the point of concurrency.

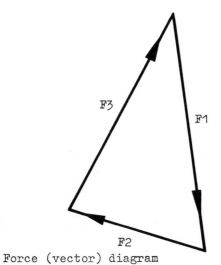

Force (vector) diagram

The force diagram is drawn to a convenient scale, so that the sides of the triangle represent the magnitude and direction of the three forces.

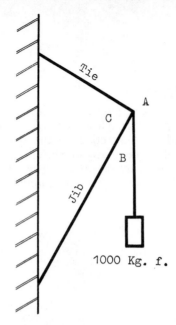

Space diagram

Frameworks

We will consider a simple wall crane, in which it is necessary to determine, graphically, the forces in the jib and tie.

Using Bow's notation, the capital letters are placed in the spaces between the forces in a clockwise direction.

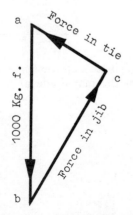

Force (vector) diagram

A suitable scale is chosen for the force diagram, and ab is drawn to represent in magnitude and direction the 1000 Kg.f. The jib bc is drawn from b in direction as the space diagram. To complete the triangle of forces the tie ca is drawn from a in direction as the space diagram.

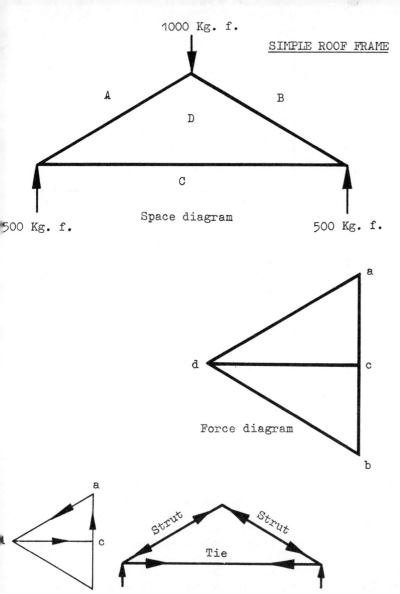

1000 Kg. f.

A

B

D

C

500 Kg. f.

Space diagram

500 Kg. f.

a

d   c

Force diagram

b

a

c

Strut   Strut

Tie

Consider a simple roof frame, in which it is necessary to determine, graphically, the magnitude and nature of the forces.

Draw the space diagram to scale showing the direction of the various members of the frame. Using Bow's notation, indicate with a capital letter the spaces between each set of forces; as there are forces acting in the members, a capital letter D is placed in the centre of the triangle. The frame is an isosceles triangle and the 1000 Kg. f. load acts at the mid-point, therefore the reactions at the supports are both 500 Kg. f.

Choose a suitable scale for the force diagram and draw the line ab to represent in magnitude and direction the 1000 Kg. f. From point b draw line bc to represent the 500 Kg. f. reaction on the right. From point c draw line ca to represent the 500 Kg. f. reaction on the left. Draw a line from a in the direction as the left-hand sloping member AD (we do not know the length of this line, for we do not yet know the magnitude of the force AD). Draw a line from b in the direction as the force BD and continue it to intersect the previous line at d. From c draw a line in the direction as the force CD (the horizontal member). This line will pass through d.

Measure ad, bd and cd to scale to obtain the force in each member.

We now, finally have to determine the nature of the forces. The direction of the left-hand reaction ca is known—upwards. Begin at c and trace a path from c to a, from a to d and then from d to c. We now transfer these arrows to the corresponding links of the space diagram as shown.

We have only dealt with the forces at the left-hand support. The above procedure must be repeated for each corner of the frame.

263

Graphical Representation of Motion

Graphical solutions are very useful when details of motion are concerned with experimental data and in cases when the motion consists of a number of distinct parts.

$$\text{Speed} = \frac{\text{distance}}{\text{time}}.$$

The units of speed are: $\dfrac{\text{metre}}{\text{second}} = \text{m/s}$, $\dfrac{\text{kilometre}}{\text{hour}} = \text{km/h}$.

$$\text{Acceleration} = \frac{\text{change of velocity}}{\text{time taken}}.$$

The problem of distinguishing between the terms speed and velocity often occurs. Speed has magnitude only, while velocity has magnitude and direction.

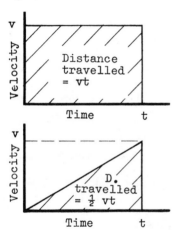

The area under a velocity-time graph gives the distance travelled. The average velocity can be obtained by dividing the area of the graph by the time interval. Acceleration is measured by the slope of the graph.

A graph of constant velocity is shown. As the slope is zero, there is no acceleration. The distance travelled $= vt$.

The graph shows uniformly accelerated motion. As the slope is constant, the acceleration is uniform. The distance travelled $=$ area of triangle $= \frac{1}{2}vt$.

A car travelling at 20 km/h accelerates uniformly to 60 km/h in 8 seconds.
The velocity-time graph is shown.
Distance travelled $=$ area under graph $=$ area of rectangle $+$ area of triangle.

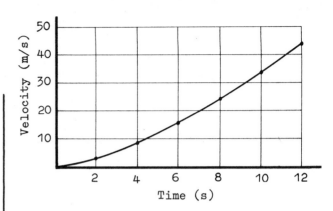

The speed of a body at a certain time is given in the accompanying table.

Time (seconds)	0	2	4	6	8	10	12
Velocity (m/s)	0	3	9	16	24	34	44

The velocity-time graph is shown above.

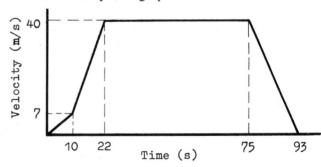

A train leaves station A and reaches a speed of 7 m/s after 10 s; it is then further accelerated during the next 12 s until a speed of 40 m/s is attained. Both the periods of acceleration are uniform.

The train maintains this speed for 53 s until station B is sighted, when the brakes are applied and the train comes to rest in 18 s with uniform retardation.

The velocity-time graph is shown above.